Amazing Math

Projects You Can Build Yourself

Numbers
GEOMETRY
Shapes

Laszlo C. Bardos

Build It Yourself Series

Nomad Press
A division of Nomad Communications
10 9 8 7 6 5 4 3 2 1

This book was manufactured by Sheridan Books,
Ann Arbor, MI USA.
July 2010, Job # 317531
ISBN: 978-1-934670-58-3

Illustrations by Samuel Carbaugh

This publication includes models from Pedagoguery Software Inc.'s Poly Pro (www.peda.com/polypro).

Questions regarding the ordering of this book should be addressed to
Independent Publishers Group
814 N. Franklin St.
Chicago, IL 60610
www.ipgbook.com

Nomad Press
2456 Christian St.
White River Junction, VT 05001
www.nomadpress.net

Other titles from Nomad Press

Contents

Introduction to Math • 1

INTRODUCTION to MATH

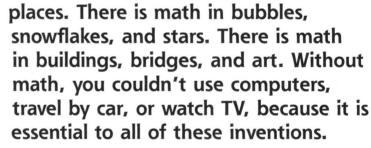

THERE IS MATH IN BUBBLES,

Grab some paper. Get out your scissors and tape. It is time to *make* some math. Yes, that's right: math is more than just a pencil-and-paper activity! In this book you will explore, create, and experiment with math. In the process, you'll find math in all sorts of unlikely places. There is math in bubbles, snowflakes, and stars. There is math in buildings, bridges, and art. Without math, you couldn't use computers, travel by car, or watch TV, because it is essential to all of these inventions.

○○○○○○○○○○○○○○○○○○○

Math exercises the logical left side of your brain. But this book will also work the right half of your brain, as you investigate patterns and seek out spatial relationships. Build the models in this book. Do the activities. You will have fun and learn more by holding these models in your hands and seeing how they work.

I hope you'll discover that math is more than just fractions and multiplication tables. It is as beautiful as a sunflower, as challenging as a puzzle, and as fun as a video game. The skills you learn in math class are vital, but not the only goal. Instead, they are tools you can use to discover, figure out, and create things.

If a topic in this book sparks your interest, please visit the companion website at **www.amazingmathprojects.com** for more information and activities. The website also has video instructions for many of the projects in this book. So if you learn better by observing, rather than reading directions, be sure to check it out.

THERE'S ALSO MATH in: Buildings, Bridges, and ART!

Project Tips

Some projects use templates that are printed in this book. You can either photocopy the templates or download templates from the website to print out. To make sturdy card stock templates, photocopy the templates onto regular paper, then staple the paper to card stock. The staples will keep the templates from moving as you cut out the pieces. When you are done, you can throw away the regular paper, and you will be left with clean card stock templates that don't have lines printed on them.

You can use recycled items from around the house for the projects. Instead of buying card stock, for example, use old manila folders. Or use empty cereal boxes for boxboard.

Numbers &
Counting

D o numbers have their own personalities? In this section you'll discover properties of numbers that set them apart from each other. Numbers can be triangular, square, or cubic. Numbers can be **prime** or **perfect.** One number is even called "golden." This number holds a special place in art and architecture and shows up in the most unlikely of places.

You might think that there is not much more to learn about counting. After all, you probably learned to count when you were very young. The way that you were taught to count is not the only way! We use 10 **digits** when we count and write numbers, but different cultures throughout history have used other systems.

In this section, we'll explore what it is like to use a system of numbers with only five digits. Computers use even fewer. They work with numbers represented by only ones and zeros.

Let's explore the world of numbers to see what surprises it has in store for us.

Did you know?

Mathematicians think that every even number greater than 2 is the sum of two prime numbers, but they aren't totally sure. Even though mathematicians used computers to verify that this is the case for every number up to one quintillion (1,000,000,000,000,000,000), they haven't proven that it works for all even numbers.

WORDS + 2 + KNOW

prime number: a number larger than 1 with only two factors: 1 and itself.

perfect number: a number whose factors (excluding the number itself) add up to that number.

factor: a number that divides evenly into another number. For example, the numbers 1, 2, 3, 4, 6, and 12 are factors of 12. To factor a number is to find the numbers that divide evenly into that number.

digit: a symbol used to write a number.

mathematician: an expert in math.

✵ Counting in Different Numeral Systems

It is so natural for us to use 10 digits to write numbers that we might not realize that there are other ways to do it. However, if we all had hands like Homer Simpson's, with only 4 fingers on each hand, we'd probably find it more natural to use 8 digits instead of 10.

oooooooooooooooooooo

In this imaginary world, we could still count as high as we wanted and add, subtract, multiply, and divide numbers using only the digits zero through seven. We might even find it easier to learn multiplication facts, because we would need to memorize up to only seven times seven!

Why doesn't it matter how many digits a number system has? The main reason is that we write numbers with place values. Each number has a ones' place, a tens' place, a hundreds' (10 x 10) place, and so on.

For example, for the number 117, there are seven elements in the ones' place, one element in the tens' place, and one element in the hundreds' place. Since each place is 10 times as great as the previous one, our system is called a **base-10** system, or a **decimal** system. The word decimal comes from the Latin word decem, which means "ten." In our imaginary world, numbers would have a ones' place, an eights' place, and a sixty-fours' (8 x 8) place. It would be a base-8, or **octal** system.

Almost 4,000 years ago, the ancient Babylonians wrote numbers in a base-60 system. To represent the number 73, for example, they drew a symbol for 1 (𒁹) next to a symbol for 13 (𒌋𒌋𒁹), showing one group of 60 plus thirteen 1s. The Babylonians' system didn't have a symbol for zero, though. So you couldn't be sure whether the symbol 𒁹 alone meant 1 or 60!

Understanding how to use number systems with different bases is important in computer programming. Computers store numbers in a base-2, or **binary**, system. The number 73, for example, is 1001001 in binary.

Base-16, or **hexadecimal**, is a system used to specify colors in web pages. The color sea green, for example, is 2E8B57 in hexadecimal. Notice the letters mixed in with the numbers. Since hexadecimal numbers use 16 digits, they use the first 6 letters of the alphabet, A–F, to represent the numbers 10–15.

Instead of using letters, we could have invented new symbols for these digits. Wouldn't it be fun to design them? What would your symbols look like?

WORDS + **2** + KNOW

base 10: a number system with 10 digits, the numbers 0 through 9.

decimal: a base-10 number system (digits 0 through 9).

octal: a base-8 number system (digits 0 through 7).

binary: a base-2 number system (digits 0 and 1), used by computers to store data.

hexadecimal: a base-16 number system (digits 0 through 9 and letters A through F).

Learn Base-5 with Money

Our system of writing numbers is called base-10 because we use 10 digits: the numbers 0 through 9. Let's try writing numbers with a base-5 system, using only the digits 0 through 4.

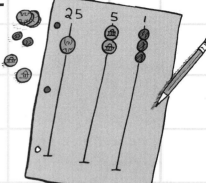

1 Draw three columns on a piece of paper. Label the first (left) column "25," the second (middle) column "5," and the third (right) column "1." Each column represents a number that is 5 times larger than the number of the column to its right.

2 Using the fewest possible coins, place quarters, nickels, and pennies in the proper columns (quarters = "25" column, nickels = "5" column, pennies = "1" column) until you have 73 cents on the paper.

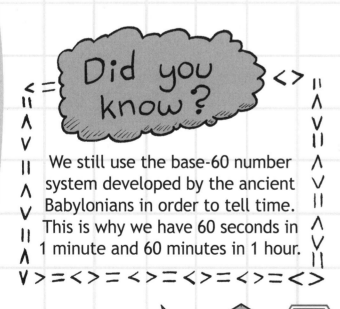

Did you know?

We still use the base-60 number system developed by the ancient Babylonians in order to tell time. This is why we have 60 seconds in 1 minute and 60 minutes in 1 hour.

Did you get 2 quarters, 4 nickels, and 3 pennies? Perfect! You just figured out how to write the number 73 in base-5: $243_{\text{base-5}}$. The base-5 in small letters tells us that the number 243 represents 2 quarters (2 x 25 = 50 cents), 4 nickels (4 x 5 = 20 cents), and 3 pennies (3 x 1 = 3 cents).

Make Base-5 Conversions

How do you represent the numbers 45 and 124 in base-5?

1 Place coins in the correct columns on the paper to figure this out. Note that you should never need more than four coins of any type. For example, if you have 5 pennies on the paper, you can replace them with 1 nickel.

2 How much money do you have if you have $314_{base\text{-}5}$?

3 What does $1000_{base\text{-}5}$ represent? Hint: you will need to add a fourth column ("125" = 25 x 5). See page 131 for the solutions to these problems.

Did you know?

In our decimal (base-10) system, it is very easy to multiply by 10: just add a zero to the end of the number that you are multiplying by 10. For example, $65 \times 10 = 650$. In a base-5 system, it is equally easy to multiply by 5: just add a zero to the end of the number you are multiplying by 5. For example, $314_{base\text{-}5}$ multiplied by 5 is $3140_{base\text{-}5}$. How would you multiply by 2 in the binary system?

Try to do some simple arithmetic entirely in base-5. For example, add $234_{base\text{-}5}$ and $142_{base\text{-}5}$. Basic addition, subtraction, multiplication, and division still work with numbers in different bases. You just need to make sure that the final number is correctly expressed in that base.

For example, $4_{base\text{-}5}$ + $2_{base\text{-}5}$ doesn't equal $6_{base\text{-}5}$ because there is no such number. Since base-5 uses only the digits 0 through 4, you write the decimal number 6 as $11_{base\text{-}5}$.

✦ Abacus

52.50?

HEY! YOU BEAT THE CALCULATOR AGAIN!

For thousands of years, people used marks in the sand, pebbles on a board, or beads on an abacus to help them add and subtract numbers. Some shopkeepers in China and Japan still use an **abacus** to calculate how much their customers owe. They do it as quickly as they could on an electronic calculator.

WORDS + **2** + KNOW

abacus: an instrument used to perform calculations by moving beads.

sorobon: a Japanese abacus.

earthly bead: a bead on an abacus with a value of 1.

heavenly bead: a bead on an abacus with a value of 5.

Did you know?

Roman numerals are tricky to work with because they don't have place values. To solve problems, the Romans translated their numerals onto an abacus, carried out the necessary calculations, and then translated the results back into Roman numerals.

Make an Abacus

You can make your own **sorobon**, a Japanese abacus. Each of the four beads closest to you has a value of 1 and is called an **earthly bead.** Each of the beads at the far end of the skewers has a value of 5 and is called a **heavenly bead.**

1 Using the nail, gently poke three evenly spaced holes near the top of each long side of the shoebox.

2 Insert one end of each skewer into a hole on one side of the box. Add four beads of one color and one of the other color to each skewer. Insert the other end of the skewer into the appropriate hole on the other side of the box. If you are using pieces of string, make sure to tie a knot at each end of the pieces once they have been inserted into the box. You want the string to be taut across the width of the box, but not so tight that it pulls the sides of the box in.

3 Push the one bead that is a different color on each skewer or string to the far side of the box and pull the four beads that are the same color to the side closest to you. Make a mark on each skewer or piece of string midway between the beads.

Supplies

- nail
- shoebox
- 15 large beads (12 of 1 color, 3 of another)
- marker
- 3 bamboo skewers or 3 pieces of string that are longer than the shoebox's short side

Use an Abacus

Place numbers onto your abacus by pushing earthly and heavenly beads toward the midway mark of the skewer. For example, the number 7 consists of 1 heavenly bead (representing 5) plus 2 earthly beads (representing 2) at the midway point. Let's add 148 and 312 on our abacus.

1 Place the number 148 on your abacus by pushing 1 earthly bead toward the midway point of the leftmost skewer (first column), 4 earthly beads towards the midway point of the middle skewer (second column), and 1 heavenly bead and 3 earthly beads to the midway point of the rightmost skewer (third column).

$$+ - \times \div \left(\sqrt{\frac{5ide}{bar^2}} \right) + - \times \div + - \times \div + - \times \div + - \times \div$$

Count to 99 on Your Fingers

Most people count to 10 on their fingers, but here is a simple way to count to 99 on your fingers. Think of your fingers as earthly beads on an abacus, with each finger having a value of 1. Your thumbs are heavenly beads, with a value of 5. Four fingers raised on your right hand represent the number 4. Your thumb and four fingers are 9. Your left hand is the tens' column, representing the numbers 10, 20, 30, and so on.

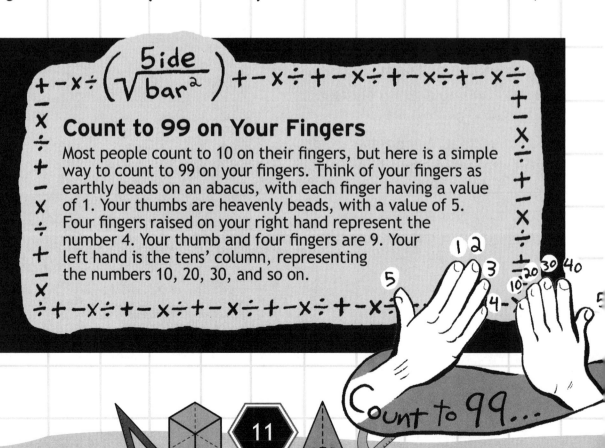

Count to 99...

11

2 To add 312, add 3 to the first column by pushing 3 more earthly beads towards the midway point. This adds 300.

3 Then, add 1 to the second column. This is a little more challenging because there are no more earthly beads left in the second column to move. To solve this problem, you will need to move the 4 earthly beads away from the midway point and bring 1 heavenly bead there. This adds 10.

4 To add 2 to the third column, you will need to "carry" a bead to the second column, because 2 + 8 equals 10. Push all beads in the rightmost column away from the midway point and add 1 earthly bead to the second column.

Read your answer by looking at the value of the beads: 460. This may seem like a difficult way to add numbers, but with practice, abacus users' motions become as automatic as typing.

⊕ -connection- ⊖

An abacus uses a mix of a base-10 system and a base-5 system. The heavenly and earthly beads represent numbers in base-5 but each column represents a base-10 place value.

✺ Triangular Numbers

SALE

On: Triangular Numbers!

Numbers can have shapes! For example, the number 10 is called a **triangular number** because you can arrange 10 pennies into the shape of an **equilateral triangle**. When you do this, each side of the triangle will be 4 pennies long.

1 penny on the top row of the triangle
2 pennies on the second row of the triangle (3 pennies total in the top 2 rows)
3 pennies on the third row of the triangle (6 pennies total in the top 3 rows)
4 pennies on the fourth row of the triangle (10 pennies total in the top 4 rows).

The first few triangular numbers, then, are 1, 3, 6, and 10.

Try It !

If 4 people each want to shake hands with every other person in the group, it will take 6 handshakes. For 5 people, it will take 10 handshakes. Both 6 and 10 are triangular numbers. Try this with a group of friends to see if you can discover why the number of handshakes is always a triangular number.

In addition to triangular numbers, there are also rectangular and square numbers, as well as numbers in many other shapes. The shape of a number reveals interesting properties, and can even make calculations easier.

Triangular numbers are associated with many different types of problems in math. For example, the total number of games in an athletic tournament, where each team plays every other team once, is a triangular number. You can also use triangular numbers to **sum** a series of **consecutive** numbers.

WORDS + 2 + KNOW

triangular number: a number of items that can be arranged into rows to form a triangle.

equilateral triangle: a triangle with all sides of equal length.

sum: the result of adding items together (the total).

consecutive: one after another in a list.

Sum a Series of Numbers

Carl Friedrich Gauss was a famous German mathematician who lived 200 years ago. When he was in elementary school, his teacher asked his class to add up all the numbers from 1 to 100, possibly to keep the class occupied for a while. However, Gauss gave the teacher the correct answer almost immediately.

Using penny triangles, we can figure out how he might have reached a solution so quickly. Look at the number of pennies in each row of the triangle. There is 1 penny in the first row, 2 in the second row, 3 in the third row, and so on. A triangle with four rows has a total of $1 + 2 + 3 + 4 = 10$ pennies in it. What does this mean? The total number of pennies in a triangle with a certain number of rows is the same as the sum of the consecutive numbers up to that number.

In this activity, instead of making a very big triangle with 100 rows of pennies and counting them all up, we'll figure out how to calculate the number of pennies in a triangle with fewer rows, and then apply that knowledge to solve our problem.

1 Create a triangle of pennies next to an upside-down triangle of nickels. Push the triangles together into a rectangle.

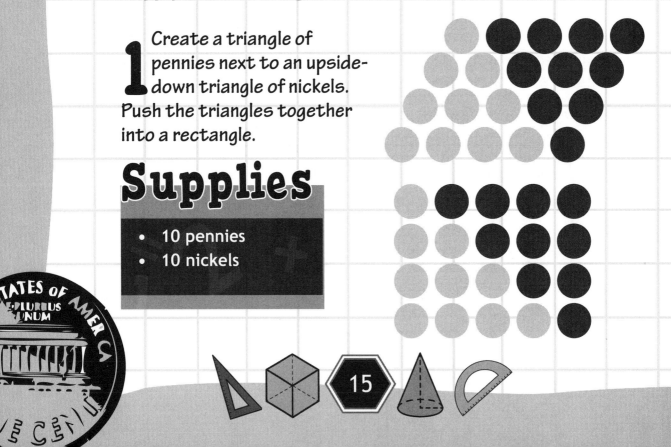

Supplies

- 10 pennies
- 10 nickels

2 Find the total number of coins in the rectangle by multiplying the number of columns by the number of rows. This is why we made a rectangle: calculating the number of coins in a rectangle is easy.

3 Divide this number by 2 in order to find the total number of pennies in your original triangle.

Count the number of rows and the number of columns in the rectangle. What do you notice? The number of columns (5) is 1 more than the number of rows (4). What does this mean? We can calculate the number of pennies in any size triangle by multiplying the number of rows by the number of columns (which is the number of rows + 1) and dividing by 2.

Returning to our original problem, what is the sum of all the numbers from 1 to 100? Again, this question is the same as asking how many pennies are in a triangle with 100 rows. Multiply the number of rows (100) by the number of columns (100 + 1 = 101) and divide by 2. 100 × 101 ÷ 2 = 5,050. This is the answer that young Gauss gave his teacher.

PUZZLE

Place 10 pennies on a table in the shape of a triangle. Moving only three pennies, turn it into a triangle that points in the opposite direction. (See page 131 for the solution.)

☸ Square Numbers

Have you ever wondered why 5 × 5 is called five **squared**? What does a square have to do with multiplication? We can find out the answer by arranging pennies into the shape of a square. A square with 5 rows and 5 columns, also called a 5 by 5 square, will have 5 × 5, or 5^2, pennies in it.

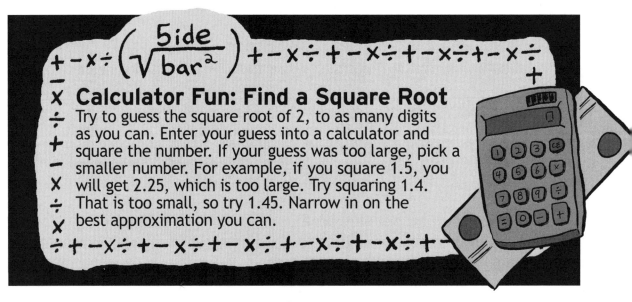

Calculator Fun: Find a Square Root

Try to guess the square root of 2, to as many digits as you can. Enter your guess into a calculator and square the number. If your guess was too large, pick a smaller number. For example, if you square 1.5, you will get 2.25, which is too large. Try squaring 1.4. That is too small, so try 1.45. Narrow in on the best approximation you can.

A number is called a **perfect square** if it is an **integer** squared. The first 12 perfect squares are 1 (1 × 1), 4 (2 × 2), 9 (3 × 3), 16 (4 × 4), 25, 36, 49, 64, 81, 100, 121, and 144.

The opposite of squaring, or multiplying a number by itself, is taking the **square root** of a number. When you take the square root of a number, you find out what number is necessary to square in order to get that number. For example, the square root of 49 is 7 because 7 × 7 = 49.

Unless a number is a perfect square, the square root of a whole number will have decimal digits that go on forever without repeating. Today, calculators quickly display approximate values for square roots that are accurate to several decimal places. For early mathematicians, square roots weren't so easy to figure out.

Mathematicians in ancient Greece had only fractions to work with, but there is no fraction that exactly equals a number like the square root of 2. For this reason these numbers are called **irrational**, a word that means "not a ratio."

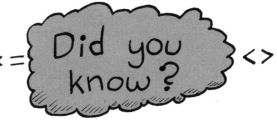

Did you know?

The sum of any two consecutive triangular numbers is a square number. For example, the triangular numbers 6 and 10 add up to 16, a perfect square. You can see why this is true by looking at this diagram. Two triangles combine to make a square.

WORDS + **2** + KNOW

square: to square a number is to multiply a number by itself. For example 5 squared (written 5^2) is 5 × 5 = 25.

perfect square: a number that is the square of an integer.

integer: a whole number, a number that does not include a fraction.

square root: a number that is squared to produce the original number. For example, the square root of 9 (written $\sqrt{9}$) is 3. $3^2 = 9$.

irrational number: a number that cannot be written as a fraction.

cube: to cube a number is to multiply a number by itself and then by itself again. For example, 4 cubed (written 4^3) is 4 × 4 × 4 = 64.

Find Patterns in Square Numbers

An interesting pattern emerges as you progress through the sequence of perfect squares. See if you can discover this pattern.

Supplies

- paper
- pencil
- approximately 25 pennies

1 Place 1 penny on a flat surface. Add 3 pennies to make a 2 by 2 square.

2 Record the number of pennies that you add each time you make a new square. For example, your list should include 1 (the number of pennies added to create the first 1 by 1 square) and 3 (the number of pennies added to create the second 2 by 2 square).

3 Add more pennies to make a 3-by-3 square. Repeat this process until you run out of pennies.

The list of numbers you wrote down should be familiar to you. First, you placed 1 penny on the surface, then you added 3, 5, and then 7 pennies. These numbers are the odd numbers. What does that mean? Perfect squares are the sum of consecutive odd numbers. If you add up the first five odd numbers, for example, you get 5 squared.

If 5 squared (5^2) is 5 × 5, then what is 5 **cubed** (5^3)? It is 5 × 5 × 5, or 5 multiplied 3 times! Five squared (25) can also be thought of as the area of a square that is 5 units wide and 5 units tall. It makes sense, then, that 5 cubed is the volume of a cube that is 5 units tall, 5 units wide, and 5 units long.

Prime Numbers ✦

Prime numbers are the building blocks of numbers. The number 7 is prime because it can be produced by the multiplication of only two whole numbers: 1 and 7. In other words, 1 and 7 are the only factors of 7.

○○○○○○○○○○○○○○○○○○○○

The number 24, on the other hand, is **composite**, not prime, because it has many factors: 1, 2, 3, 4, 6, 8, 12, and 24. The first few prime numbers are 2, 3, 5, 7, 11, 13, 17, 19, 23, 29, 31, and 37. Notice that 1, by definition, is not prime, and that 2 is the only even prime number.

WORDS + **2** + KNOW

prime number: a number larger than 1 with only two factors: 1 and itself. The number 1 is not a prime number.

composite: any number greater than 1 that is not a prime number.

⊕ -connection- ⊖

Rectangular Numbers

If you were to arrange a prime number of pennies in rows and columns on a table, you could place the pennies all in a row, but you couldn't arrange them into any other rectangle.

Find Prime Numbers

Here is an easy way to find all the prime numbers between 1 and 100. Eratosthenes, a mathematician from ancient Greece, invented this method around 200 BCE. It is called the **Sieve of Eratosthenes** because it filters out prime numbers from a list in much the same way that a sieve filters out pebbles from a pile of sand.

1 Draw a 10 by 10 grid. List the numbers from 1 to 100 in the boxes of the grid. Cross off the number 1 because by definition it isn't prime.

2 Circle the number 2 and then cross off every number greater than 2 that is divisible by 2 (4, 6, 8, etc.). The number 2 is the only prime number that is even.

Supplies

- pencil
- paper

WORDS + 2 + KNOW

Sieve of Eratosthenes: a method for finding prime numbers.

perfect number: a number whose factors (excluding the number itself) add up to that number.

X̶	②	3	X̶	5	X̶	7	X̶	9	X̶1̶0̶
11	X̶1̶2̶	13	X̶1̶4̶	15	...	...	...	...	...
...	...	...	...	...	...	...	...	...	...
...	...	...	...	...	...	...	...	...	...
...	...	...	...	...	...	...	...	...	...
...	...	...	...	...	...	...	...	...	...
...	...	...	...	...	...	...	...	...	...
...	...	...	...	...	...	...	...	...	...
...	...	...	...	...	...	...	...	...	...
...	...	...	...	...	...	...	...	...	...
...	...	...	...	...	...	...	...	...	...

21

3 Circle the number 3 and cross off every third number after that. Some of these numbers will be crossed off already. This step removes all the numbers divisible by 3, which we know can't be prime. Repeat with the numbers 5 and 7.

4 Circle every number not crossed off. The circled numbers are all the prime numbers between 1 and 100.

PUZZLE

The number 6 is a "**perfect number**" because its factors, excluding itself (1, 2, 3), add up to 6. The number 496 is also a perfect number because its factors, excluding itself, (1, 2, 4, 8, 16, 31, 62, 124, and 248) add up to 496. Can you find the only perfect number between these two numbers? Hint 1: It is between 20 and 30. Hint 2: All perfect numbers are also triangular numbers! (See page 131 for the solution.)

You may be wondering why we didn't look for multiples of 11, 13, or greater prime numbers. Couldn't some of the remaining numbers have 11 as a factor? A quick look at the chart will convince you that all multiples of 11 (22, 33, 44, etc.) have been crossed off already. We eliminated them when we dealt with the smaller prime numbers. On a chart with 100 numbers, we need to check primes only up to 10, the square root of 100. On any chart, stop checking primes when you reach the square root of its largest number.

✿Fractions

Today, we express parts of a whole in three different ways: through fractions, decimals, and percents. However, if you were doing math in ancient Egypt or ancient Greece, you would have worked in fractions only. Decimals and percents didn't really catch on until a thousand years later.

ooooooooooooooooooo

Adding and multiplying fractions can be tricky. Here are a couple of activities that will help you see the concepts behind adding and multiplying fractions.

Multiply Fractions

You don't need to find a common denominator to multiply fractions.

Supplies

- graph paper
- colored pencils or crayons

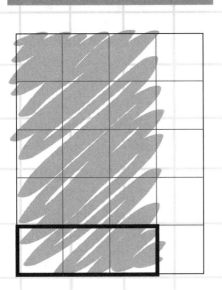

1 To multiply ¾ x ⅕, draw a rectangle 4 squares across (4 columns) by 5 squares down (5 rows). The number of rows and columns are the denominators of the two fractions.

2 Color ¾ of the rectangle, or 3 of the 4 columns. With a different color, shade ⅕ of the part you just colored, or 1 of the 5 rows of already shaded squares.

3 Find the answer by counting squares that are shaded twice, which represent ⅕ of ¾. Three out of the 20 squares in the rectangle are shaded twice, so the answer is ³/₂₀ .

The first step of this activity shows that multiplying fractions involves multiplying denominators. The 4 in ¾ times the 5 in ⅕ equals 20 squares. The key to this method, and being able to take a fraction of a fraction, is to have the right number of squares in the rectangle starting out. Setting the dimensions of the rectangle to the values of the two denominators ensures that we can divide the rectangle evenly in the next step.

Your finished diagram also shows you that you multiply numerators when you multiply fractions. The doubly shaded part is one numerator wide by the other numerator long. The area of this part is the product of the numerators, the 3 in ¾ times the 1 in ⅕ .

Make a Fraction Addition Dial

In this activity, you'll create a simple tool to help you add fractions. We'll practice by adding the fractions $\frac{3}{8}$ and $\frac{1}{6}$.

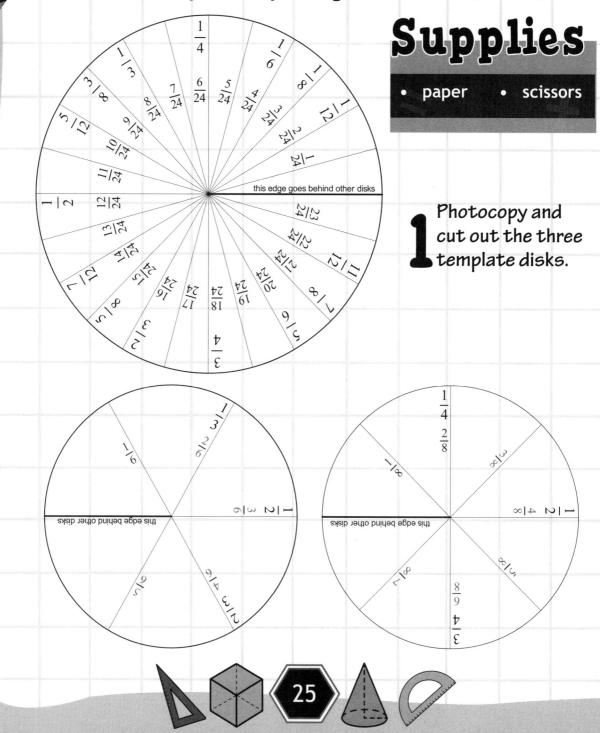

this edge goes behind other disks

Supplies

- paper
- scissors

1 Photocopy and cut out the three template disks.

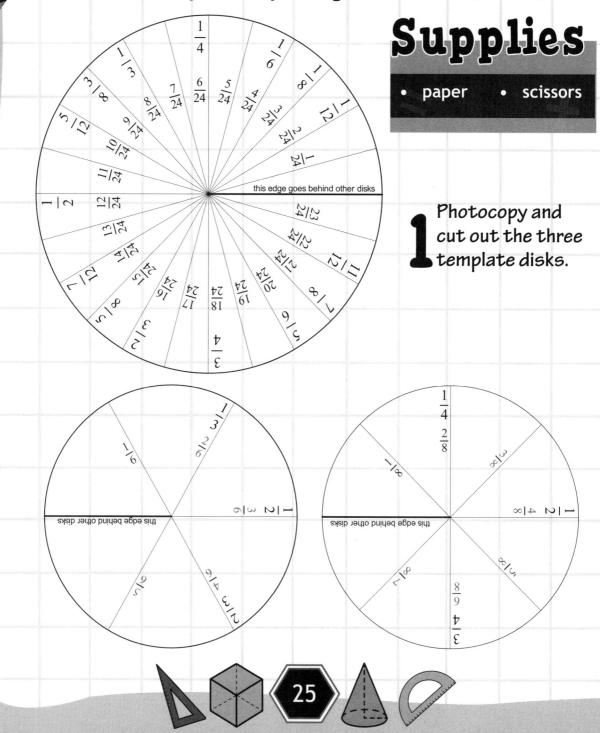

this edge behind other disks

this edge behind other disks

2 Cut a slit in each disk from the edge to the center of the circle along the thick line.

3 Slip the two smaller disks onto the larger one at the slits. Place the disk divided into eighths on top of the one divided into sixths.

4 To add the fractions ³⁄₈ and ¹⁄₆, rotate the top disk until the fraction ³⁄₈ is showing.

5 Rotate the second disk so that the fraction ¹⁄₆ lines up with the end of the top disk. In other words, the second disk sticks out from under the top disk by ¹⁄₆.

6 Read the answer ¹³⁄₂₄ off of the bottom circle where the second disk ends.

The fraction dial illustrates why you need to get common denominators to add fractions. If the bottom disk had only eighths and sixths marked on it, the answer would fall between two lines. You wouldn't be able to read the answer. Here we have more lines, showing 24ths, which is the common denominator.

✦Fibonacci Sequence

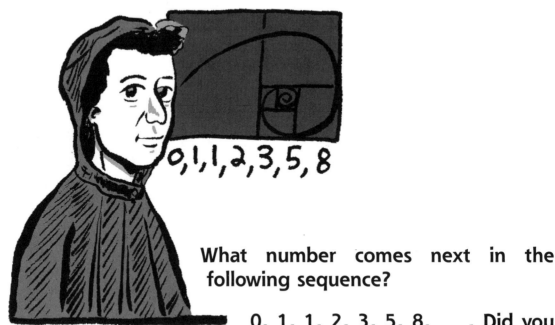

0, 1, 1, 2, 3, 5, 8

What number comes next in the following sequence?

0, 1, 1, 2, 3, 5, 8, ___. Did you figure it out? The next number is 13. Why? Each new number in the sequence is the sum of the two numbers before it. To find the next number in this sequence, then, you needed to add the two previous numbers, 5 and 8.

○○○○○○○○○○○○○○○○○○

Here is the sequence with a few more numbers: 0, 1, 1, 2, 3, 5, 8, 13, 21, 34, 55, 89, 144, 233, 377, 610, 987, 1597, 2584, 4181, 6765, ...

This pattern of numbers is called the **Fibonacci sequence**, after a nickname given to a man named Leonardo of Pisa. He was an Italian mathematician who included it in a book he wrote in the year 1202. The nickname is short for filius Bonacci, meaning "son of the Bonacci family."

WORDS + **2** + KNOW

Fibonacci sequence: a series of numbers formed by adding the previous two numbers to get the next one.

Make a
Square Magically Appear

Amaze your friends with this fun trick that uses Fibonacci numbers!

Supplies

- graph paper
- pencil
- scissors

1 Cut out an 8 by 8 square of graph paper. Cut the square into pieces along the thick lines shown.

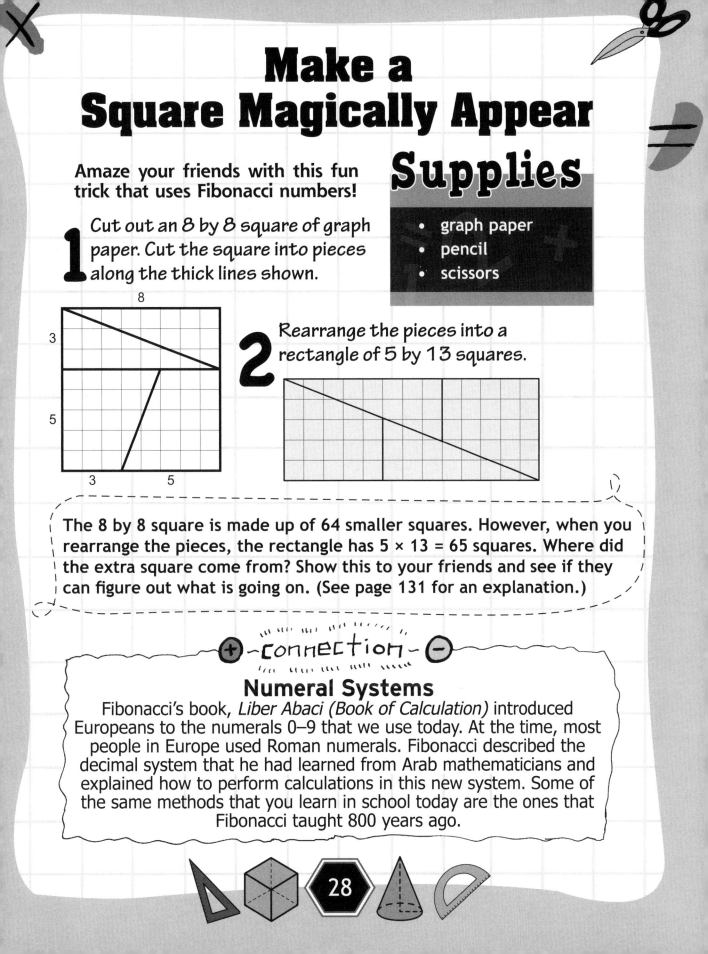

2 Rearrange the pieces into a rectangle of 5 by 13 squares.

The 8 by 8 square is made up of 64 smaller squares. However, when you rearrange the pieces, the rectangle has 5 × 13 = 65 squares. Where did the extra square come from? Show this to your friends and see if they can figure out what is going on. (See page 131 for an explanation.)

⊕ -connection- ⊖

Numeral Systems

Fibonacci's book, *Liber Abaci (Book of Calculation)* introduced Europeans to the numerals 0–9 that we use today. At the time, most people in Europe used Roman numerals. Fibonacci described the decimal system that he had learned from Arab mathematicians and explained how to perform calculations in this new system. Some of the same methods that you learn in school today are the ones that Fibonacci taught 800 years ago.

Find Spirals in a Sunflower

The numbers of the Fibonnaci sequence appear in some surprising places, including nature. For example, look at the pattern of the seeds in the center of this sunflower. The seeds arrange themselves in spirals radiating out from the center. Similar patterns of spirals occur in the center of daisies, on the bottom of pine cones, and in the bumps of a pineapple.

At first, it may appear that the spirals turn in only one direction. However, if you look closely, you will notice that there are two sets of intertwining spirals: some turning right and some turning left.

Can you find the spirals in this drawing of sunflower seeds?

Supplies

- colored pencils or crayons

1 Connect the dots to form spirals. Use one color for spirals turning in one direction and another color for spirals turning in the other direction.

2 Don't worry if you can't follow the spirals all the way to the center: it gets a little more complicated there. When you are done coloring, count the number of spirals of each color.

The remarkable thing about these spirals is that you'll find a Fibonacci number of them. For example, on a pine cone, there may be 8 spirals turning in one direction, and 13 turning in the other.

On a pineapple, you might be able to find three sets of spirals: 5, 8 and 13 of each type. The next time you see a pineapple or a pine cone, see if you can find their spirals.

PUZZLE

Look again at the drawing of sunflower seeds. There are more spirals than the two kinds you colored. See if you can find other spirals in the drawing. (See page 131 for the solution.)

✦ Golden Ratio

Golden Ratio 1.61803

Use a calculator to divide two consecutive numbers in the Fibonacci sequence. For example, try dividing 13 by 8. Now try dividing larger consecutive numbers in the sequence. Do you see a pattern? The results of these divisions are all slightly greater than 1.6. As you divide larger and larger pairs of numbers in the Fibonacci sequence, their ratio comes even closer to 1.61803, closing in on a special number. This number is called the golden ratio. It is one of the few numbers lucky enough to get its own Greek letter. It is often referred to as phi (pronounced "fie" and rhymes with pie) and the Greek letter looks like this: φ.

ooooooooooooooooooooo

The golden ratio has fascinated people for centuries. For example, some architects and artists use it in their work. They may design a rectangle φ times as wide as it is tall, a so-called **golden rectangle**, because they think it has a pleasing shape.

The golden ratio has even been called the "divine proportion." People have searched for the golden ratio in all sorts of places: in the dimensions of the human body, in the spiral of a shell, even in patterns in the stock market. Historians have looked for the golden ratio in famous paintings like the Mona Lisa and in the design of ancient Greek buildings. No one knows for sure whether the golden ratios found in these places are there by chance or if they were deliberately included, but it is fun to guess.

WORDS + **2** + KNOW

ratio: a comparison of two numbers or measurements, dividing one number by another.

golden ratio: the number $(1+\sqrt{5}) \div 2$ or approximately 1.61803, sometimes represented by the Greek letter φ.

golden rectangle: a rectangle with a ratio of its length to width of φ to 1.

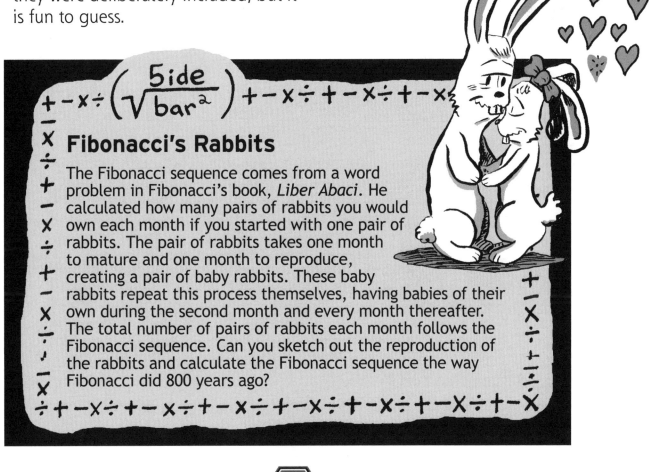

$$+-\times\div\left(\sqrt{\frac{5ide}{bar^2}}\right)+-\times\div+-\times\div+-\times$$

Fibonacci's Rabbits

The Fibonacci sequence comes from a word problem in Fibonacci's book, *Liber Abaci*. He calculated how many pairs of rabbits you would own each month if you started with one pair of rabbits. The pair of rabbits takes one month to mature and one month to reproduce, creating a pair of baby rabbits. These baby rabbits repeat this process themselves, having babies of their own during the second month and every month thereafter. The total number of pairs of rabbits each month follows the Fibonacci sequence. Can you sketch out the reproduction of the rabbits and calculate the Fibonacci sequence the way Fibonacci did 800 years ago?

Find the Golden Ratio Around You

more on the Web

You can check objects around you to see if they contain the golden ratio by making these golden ratio dividers. When you open the dividers, the middle pointer will divide the opening into two parts with the larger part φ times as long as the shorter part. (The full span of the dividers is also φ times as large as the larger part.)

1 Photocopy and cut out the four pieces from the template to the right.

2 With a craft knife, cut out the holes and cut along the lines that form the tabs.

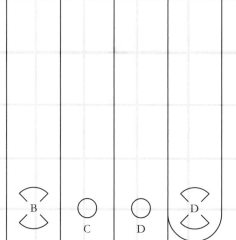

3 Lift up and curl in the tabs so that they fit through the holes.

33

4 Slip the tabs marked "A" through the hole marked "A" and flatten the tabs once they are through the hole. Assemble the rest of the pieces in the same way, matching the tabs with the holes marked with the same letter.

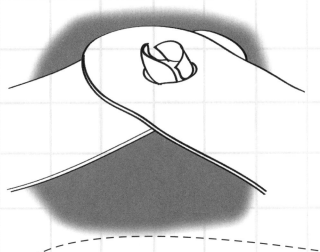

5 Find a photo of your favorite celebrity on the Internet. Hold the dividers up to the photo to see if this person has golden ratios hidden in the proportions of their face. Open the dividers so that the longer part measures the height of the face. Now check to see if the width of the face is the length of the shorter part. If so, the person's face is φ times as long as it is wide. Does the nose split the distance between the eyes and the chin in the golden ratio?

You can look for the golden ratio in other places as well. Look in the shapes of buildings, the layout of artwork, the shapes of leaves, and the lengths of the bones in your hand. Happy hunting!

Let's go back to the sunflower. Why do the Fibonacci numbers appear there? A sunflower plant packs as many seeds as possible into its flower. Each new seed grows a certain angle away from the previous seed. The angle that allows the most seeds to fit is an angle based on the golden ratio. Each seed is φ revolutions away from the one before it, about 222.5 degrees. Since Fibonacci numbers are related to the golden ratio, they appear as spirals.

Draw a Golden Spiral

If you cut a square off of a golden rectangle, you are left with a smaller golden rectangle. If you continue doing this, you will keep producing smaller and smaller golden rectangles. We'll use this pattern to create a golden spiral.

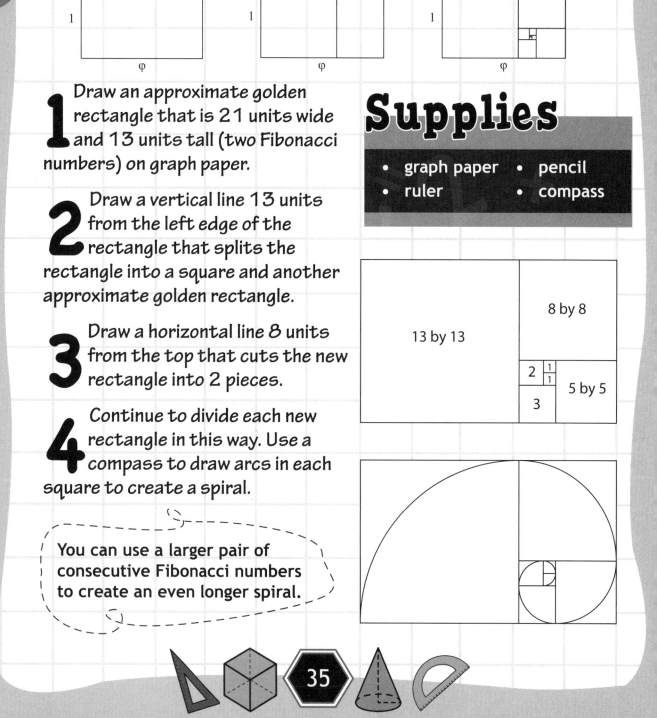

1 Draw an approximate golden rectangle that is 21 units wide and 13 units tall (two Fibonacci numbers) on graph paper.

2 Draw a vertical line 13 units from the left edge of the rectangle that splits the rectangle into a square and another approximate golden rectangle.

3 Draw a horizontal line 8 units from the top that cuts the new rectangle into 2 pieces.

4 Continue to divide each new rectangle in this way. Use a compass to draw arcs in each square to create a spiral.

You can use a larger pair of consecutive Fibonacci numbers to create an even longer spiral.

Supplies

- graph paper
- ruler
- pencil
- compass

13 by 13

8 by 8

5 by 5

2

1
1

3

Angles, Curves, and Paths

Did you know that most things are made of angles and curves?

Yeah! Like suspension bridges.

We see lines and angles all around us in manmade items. Nature, on the other hand, is filled with curves. In this section, we'll marvel at the graceful path that a baseball takes when it is thrown into the air. We'll see how this curve is related to other curves like the path of a planet's orbit around the sun. Finally, we'll analyze all sorts of paths, from the route of a person taking a stroll to the chaotic path of a randomly moving molecule.

✪ Angles

Two lines that meet at a point form angles. Angles are used everywhere. Carpenters use angles to cut wood accurately. Civil engineers use angles to construct roads. Astronomers use angles to locate stars in the sky. Angles are a way to measure and describe shapes.

The angle you see the most in architecture is a 90-degree angle, called a **right angle**. The ancient Egyptians who built the Great Pyramid of Giza needed to make accurate right angles in the pyramid's square base. How did ancient Egyptians measure right angles? While no one knows for sure, many historians believe they used a triangle made of rope.

WORDS + 2 + KNOW

right angle: a 90-degree angle.

right triangle: a triangle with a right angle in it.

leg: either of the two shorter sides of a right triangle.

hypotenuse: the longest side of a right triangle.

Pythagorean theorem: an equation relating the side lengths of a right triangle.

Find Right Angles

In this activity, you can try out the Egyptian's method of measuring right angles yourself!

1 Mark the string with a marker every 4 inches (10 centimeters) until you have made 13 marks.

2 Tie the string into a loop so that the first and last marks meet at the knot. Tape the knot down onto a flat surface.

3 Count four marks, stretch the string tight in any direction, and tape the mark down onto the flat surface.

4 Count three more marks, stretch the string tight, and tape the mark down onto the flat surface. Each side of the triangle should now be tight.

Supplies

- 5 feet of string
- marker
- ruler
- tape

You just created a **right triangle** like the ones the Egyptians may have used to build the pyramids. You can use the right angle at the corner of this book to see how close the angle in your rope triangle is to 90 degrees.

So why does the rope triangle make a right angle? Count the number of marks to see how long each side of the triangle is. One **leg** of the triangle is three marks long, the other leg is four, and the longest side (the **hypotenuse**) is five. The **Pythagorean theorem** tells us that if you square the lengths of the two legs of a right triangle and add the results together, you will get the square of the length of the hypotenuse. If you use the letters a and b for the lengths of the legs and the letter c for the length of the hypotenuse, the equation looks like this: $a^2 + b^2 = c^2$.

Try putting the numbers 3, 4, and 5 into this equation to see that it really does work. Does $3^2 + 4^2 = 5^2$?

Illustrate the Supplies

There are many different ways to show that the Pythagorean theorem works. Here is a simple way, developed by the mathematician Thābit ibn Qurra in Baghdad over 1,000 years ago.

Supplies

• scissors • paper

1 Photocopy and cut out the template shapes. These are Pythagorean theorem puzzle pieces. The two right triangles have side lengths of a, b, and c.

2 Arrange the pieces to fit into the first shape. This pattern forms two squares with areas of a^2 and b^2.

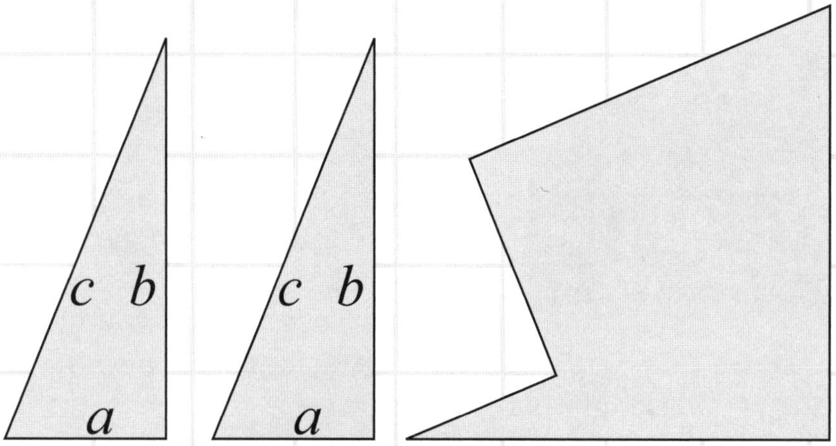

c b

a

c b

a

Did you know?

Even though the Pythagorean theorem is named after the Greek mathematician Pythagoras, he wasn't the first to discover it. Mathematicians in ancient Babylon calculated the side lengths of right triangles 1,000 years before he did.

Pythagorean Theorem

3 Using the same pieces, arrange them to fit the square with area c^2. You just showed that a^2 plus b^2 equals c^2.

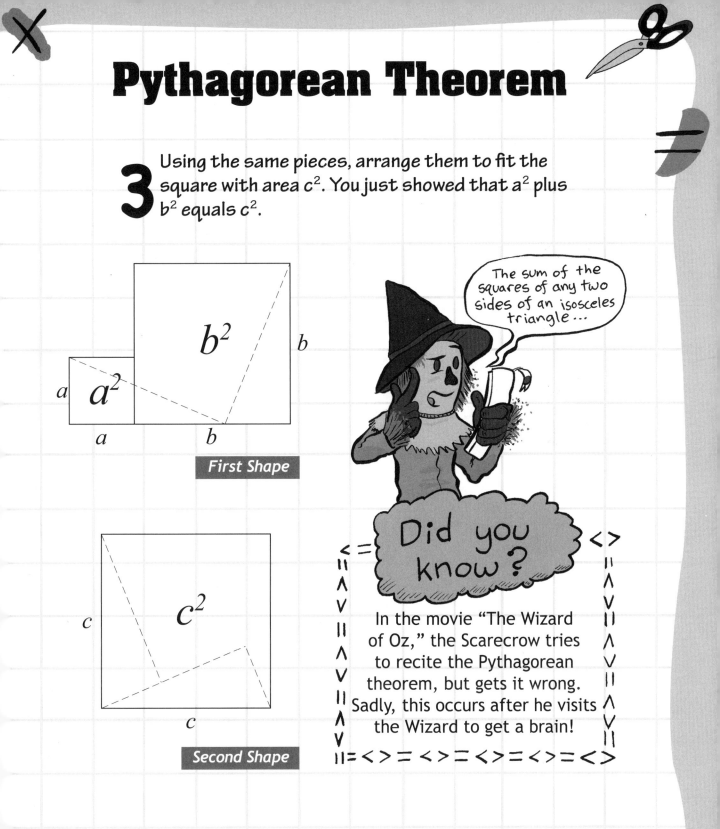

b^2

b

a a^2

a

b

First Shape

c c^2

c

Second Shape

The sum of the squares of any two sides of an isosceles triangle...

Did you know?

In the movie "The Wizard of Oz," the Scarecrow tries to recite the Pythagorean theorem, but gets it wrong. Sadly, this occurs after he visits the Wizard to get a brain!

Measure Angles with an Inclinometer

more on the Web

On a piece of paper, you can measure angles using a **protractor**. But how do you measure how steep a ski slope is or how high in the sky the moon is? In this activity, you will create a model of an **inclinometer**, a tool that measures angles like these.

Supplies

- paper
- scissors
- pushpin
- string
- tape
- washer
- thread
- cardboard tube (from an empty roll of paper towels)

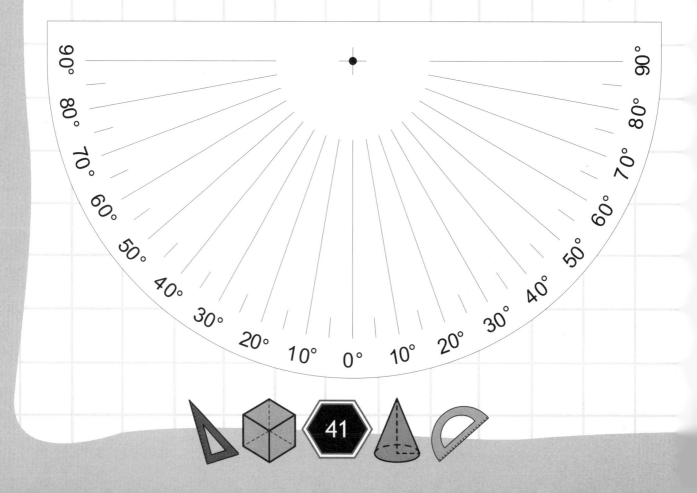

1 Photocopy and cut out the template. Use the pushpin to poke a hole at the dot, and then slip the string through the hole. Tape the end of the string to the back of the scale.

2 Tie a washer onto the other end of the string so that the washer hangs below the scale. Tape the scale to the bottom of the tube.

3 Cut a short slit on the top, bottom, left, and right sides at one end of the cardboard tube.

4 Slip the thread into the slits to form crosshairs in the tube and tape the thread in place.

5 Measure an angle by looking through the tube toward the object you would like to measure. When the washer stops swaying, pinch the string against the scale to hold it in place. Read the angle of the string on the scale.

WORDS + 2 + KNOW

protractor: a device for drawing and measuring angles.

inclinometer: an instrument for measuring angles.

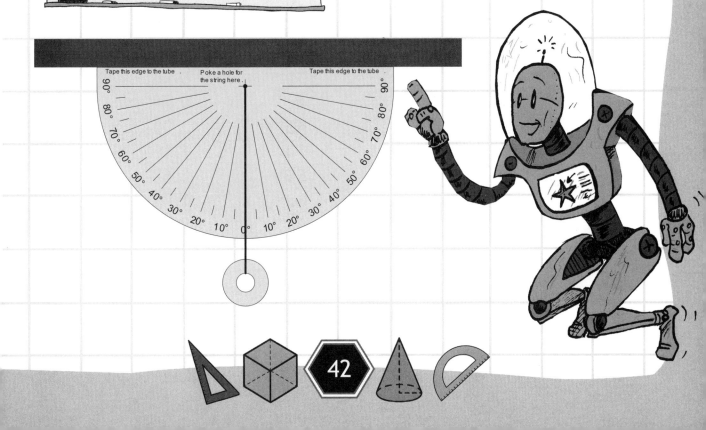

Tape this edge to the tube   Poke a hole for   Tape this edge to the tube
the string here
90° 80° 70° 60° 50° 40° 30° 20° 10° 0° 10° 20° 30° 40° 50° 60° 70° 80° 90°

Find the Height of a Tree

Your inclinometer can help you measure
how tall a tree is without climbing it.

1 Measure the angle to the top of the tree with your inclinometer. Measure how far away from the tree you are standing, as well as how high above the ground your inclinometer is when you use it.

2 In the table, find the row with the angle that is closest to the angle you measured. Multiply your distance from the tree by the number in the second column of the row. (If you have a scientific calculator you can find the multiplier for your angle by entering the angle and pushing the button TAN. TAN is short for tangent.)

Angle	Multiply by
20°	0.36
25°	0.47
30°	0.58
35°	0.70
40°	0.84
45°	1.00
50°	1.19
55°	1.43
60°	1.73
65°	2.14
70°	2.75

Did you know?

You can approximate how high in the sky the moon is by holding your arm straight out in front of you and making a fist. Your fist is approximately 10 degrees from top to bottom. Count how many fists above the horizon the moon is.

Supplies

- inclinometer from the previous activity
- tape measure

3 Add the height your inclinometer was above the ground to the number you calculated in step 2 to get the height of the tree.

y ft

x ft

✪ Parabola

When you toss a ball into the air, the path it takes is a very graceful up-and-down curve called a **parabola**. This remarkable curve appears in many places in nature and in many objects made by humans. It is the shape made by water streaming out of a drinking fountain, as well as the shape of the cable on a suspension bridge.

ooooooooooooooooooo

When you stir a glass of water, the surface of the water forms a **concave** shape called a **paraboloid**, which is a three-dimensional version of a parabola. Telescope mirrors, satellite dishes, and reflectors on super-sensitive microphones all take the form of paraboloids, because they are able to reflect waves coming from far away to a single point, called the **focus**.

WORDS + 2 + KNOW

parabola: a U-shaped curve that is a cross section of a cone.

concave: curved inward like a bowl or the letter "C."

paraboloid: a dish-shaped surface made by rotating a parabola.

focus (of a parabola): the point inside a parabolic reflector where incoming light rays meet.

vertex (of a parabola): the lowest point of a parabola that opens up like a "U."

catenary: a curve that is the shape of a hanging chain.

Parabolas are made up of square numbers. To draw a simple parabola on a piece of graph paper, draw one dot where you want the bottom of the parabola to be. This spot is called the **vertex**. Draw a second dot 1 grid mark to the right and 1 grid mark up (1^2) from the vertex. Draw a third dot 2 grid marks to the right and 4 grid marks up (2^2) from the vertex.

Continue drawing dots on the right side following this rule: however many units you move to the right, move up that number squared. Then repeat this process on the left side of the vertex. Connect the dots on both sides with a smooth curve.

Did you know?

Hold a piece of rope by each end and let it sag in the middle. This curve looks like a parabola, but actually it is a slightly different curve called a **catenary**. Don't worry if you can't tell the difference. Even the great Galileo mistakenly thought that a hanging rope formed a parabola. This curve is an excellent shape for making a strong arch. The Gateway Arch in St. Louis is in the shape of an upside-down catenary. Thomas Jefferson, our third president, invented the word catenary. It comes from the Latin word for chain.

Fold a Parabola

Supplies

* paper
* pencil

You can make a parabola out of the creases on a piece of paper.

1 Draw a dot on a piece of paper about 2 inches (5 centimeters) above the middle of the bottom edge.

2 Fold the paper so that the bottom edge of the paper touches the dot. Unfold the paper after you have left a clear crease.

3 Make many more creases, touching a different location on the bottom edge to the dot each time. The creases form a parabola.

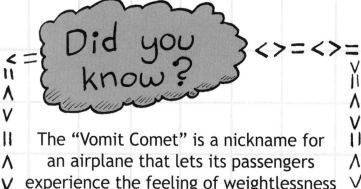

Did you know?

The "Vomit Comet" is a nickname for an airplane that lets its passengers experience the feeling of weightlessness for about 25 seconds at a time. This airplane travels a parabolic path to simulate this condition.

more on the Web

Record a Parabolic Arc

The path of an object tossed into the air is a parabola. It can be difficult to see this, however, because the motion happens so fast. In this activity, you will record and study the parabolic path formed by a ball rolling on a ramp.

1 Cover a large section of the floor with newspaper.

2 Create a shallow ramp by leaning the piece of cardboard or wooden board on a stack of bricks. For example, raise the end of a board that is 3 feet long (1 meter) about 1 foot high (30 centimeters). Place a large piece of paper on the ramp.

Supplies

- newspaper
- large piece of cardboard or a wooden board
- several bricks
- paint
- large pieces of paper (such as posterboard or flip-chart paper)
- tennis ball

3 Practice rolling the tennis ball up the paper-covered ramp at an angle so that it forms a nice arc on the ramp and rolls back down again.

4 Now cover the tennis ball with paint. Repeat step 3 with the paint-covered ball. Try rolling different parabolas, some skinny and some fat.

✿ Ellipses

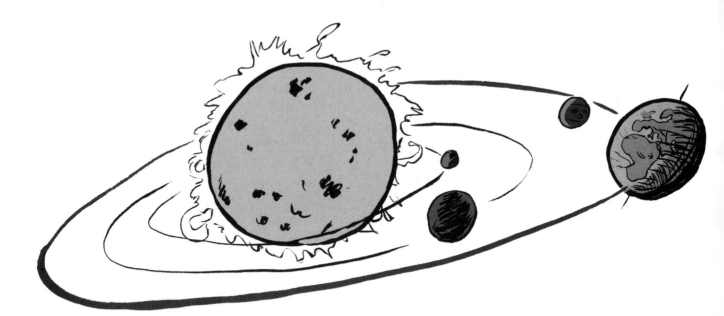

The earth travels around the sun in an orbit that is nearly, but not quite, a circle. In January, we are a little closer to the sun than we are in July. The shape of our orbit is an **ellipse**, which is the mathematical term for an oval.

WORDS + 2 + KNOW

ellipse: an oval-shaped curve that is a cross-section of a cone.

cross section: the two-dimensional shape you would see if you were to cut a three-dimensional object in two with one straight cut.

focus (of an ellipse): the points that define an ellipse. Waves that start at one focus and reflect inside an ellipse meet at the other focus. The plural of focus is foci.

The earth not only has an elliptical orbit, it also has an elliptical shape, bulging in the middle. If you cut the earth in half from pole to pole, you would see an elliptical **cross section**.

The easiest way to see an ellipse is to hold a glass of water at an angle. The surface of the water forms an ellipse in the glass.

Draw an Ellipse

Supplies

- tape
- paper
- cardboard
- two pushpins
- string
- pencil

1 Tape a piece of paper onto the cardboard. Push two pushpins into the middle of the paper, about 6 inches (15 centimeters) apart from each other.

2 Tie about 16 inches (40 centimeters) of string into a loop and place the loop loosely around the pushpins.

3 Hook the end of the pencil into the loop and pull the string taut.

4 Draw with the pencil around the pushpins, keeping the string tight the whole time.

Each pushpin marks a **focus** of the ellipse. Try drawing another ellipse with the pushpins set farther apart. What happens to the shape of the ellipse? What shape would you get if you used only one pushpin?

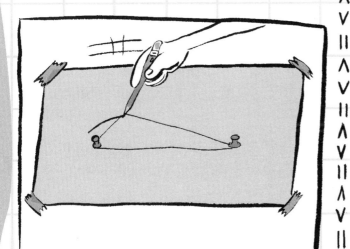

Did you know?

Whispering galleries in science museums and other locations are shaped like ellipses. In these rooms, you can whisper something very quietly at one end, and have another person at the other end hear you clearly. Your voice travels out from one focus of the ellipse, reflects against the walls, and arrives at the other focus.

❂ Cutting a Cone

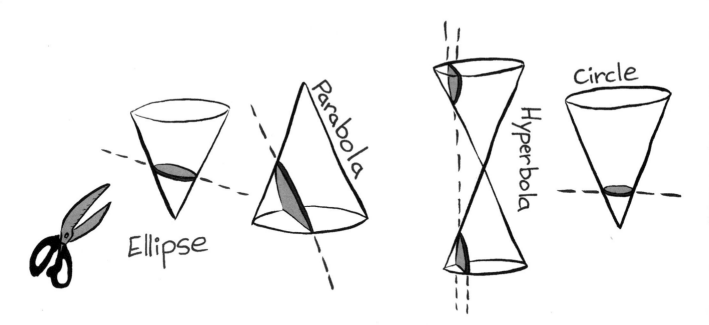

Parabola

Ellipse

Hyperbola

Circle

What does a parabola have in common with a circle and an ellipse? All three of these curves can be made by cutting a cone in different ways, called conic sections.

ooooooooooooooooooooo

If you cut a cone horizontally at its tip, you will see a surface in the shape of a circle. Likewise, if you cut it slantwise at its tip, you will reveal an ellipse. Furthermore, if you cut it at an even steeper slant across the cone— at the same angle as the side of the cone—you will produce a parabola.

WORDS + **2** + KNOW

conic section: a curve that is a cross section of a cone: a circle, ellipse, parabola, or hyperbola.

hyperbola: a curve with two branches formed by cutting a double cone.

Finally, if you cut it any steeper, you will get yet another curve: a **hyperbola**. A hyperbola has two branches, so you need to cut two cones placed tip to tip to see both parts of the curve.

Explore Conic Sections

more on the Web

Supplies

- card stock
- scissors
- glue

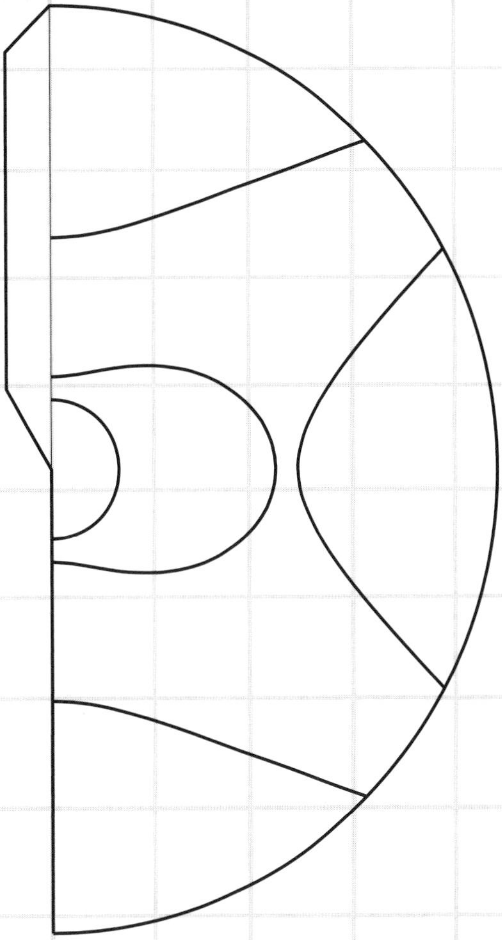

1 Photocopy and cut out the templates from card stock.

2 Roll the first one up into a cone and glue (or tape) the tab to the other edge.

3 Cut out the circle and ellipse from the second template.

4 Place this template on the cone in different orientations to see how it cuts a cone into the different conic sections.

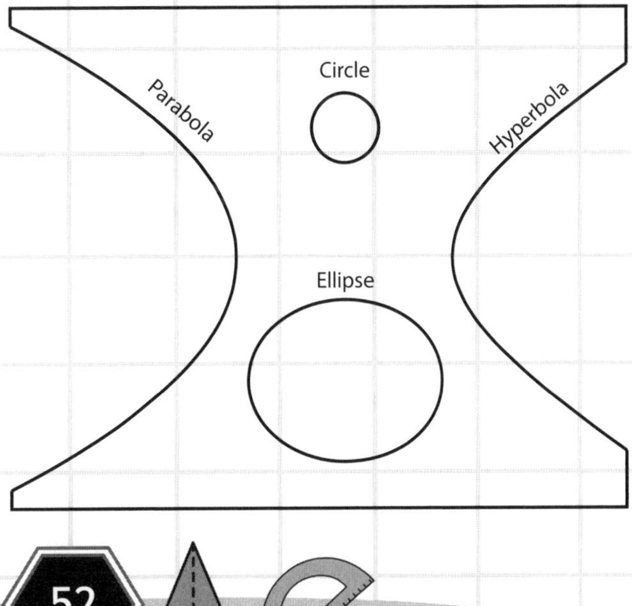

Parabola

Circle

Hyperbola

Ellipse

52

✿ Paths

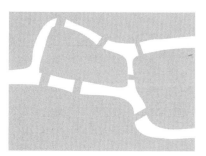

The old German town of Königsberg had seven bridges connecting two islands and the shores of the river Pregel. Leonard Euler, the great mathematician, was given the problem of determining whether it was possible to take a walk that crosses each bridge only once.

Here is a simple map of the bridges of Königsberg. Try drawing a path that crosses each of the seven bridges only once without lifting your pencil.

○○○○○○○○○○○○○○○○○○○○○

Give up? No surprise: the task is impossible! Most likely, the citizens of Königsberg tried to solve the problem enough times to suspect that their search for a solution was hopeless.

Why was Euler interested in this seemingly simple problem? He was an important mathematician, the head of the mathematics department of St. Petersburg Academy of Sciences. Euler recognized that this was a completely new type of problem for mathematicians.

Through his work on the problem, Euler created a totally new field of mathematics that has a wide range of applications today. The techniques used to solve problems like this one are crucial to analyzing Internet connections. They are used to find the shortest route between points, analyze traffic flow, and design printed circuit boards for electronics.

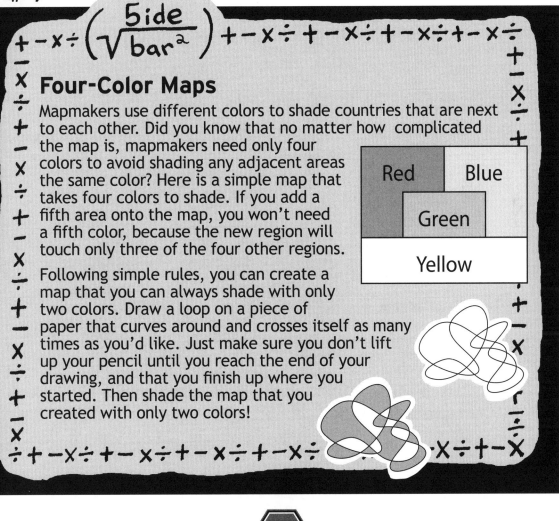

Four-Color Maps

Mapmakers use different colors to shade countries that are next to each other. Did you know that no matter how complicated the map is, mapmakers need only four colors to avoid shading any adjacent areas the same color? Here is a simple map that takes four colors to shade. If you add a fifth area onto the map, you won't need a fifth color, because the new region will touch only three of the four other regions.

Following simple rules, you can create a map that you can always shade with only two colors. Draw a loop on a piece of paper that curves around and crosses itself as many times as you'd like. Just make sure you don't lift up your pencil until you reach the end of your drawing, and that you finish up where you started. Then shade the map that you created with only two colors!

Red	Blue
Green	
Yellow	

The problem of Königsberg's bridges is made easier if you draw a very simple diagram: essentially, a stick figure. Instead of drawing islands and bridges, we'll draw dots with lines connecting them. Each dot, called a **vertex**, is a landing place, while each line, called an **edge**, is a bridge.

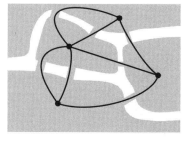

WORDS + 2 + KNOW

vertex (of a graph): a dot on a graph that represents a place or a thing that you are studying. The plural of vertex is vertices.

edge (of a graph): a line that connects two vertices of a graph that represents their relationship.

graph: a diagram used to analyze the relationships or connections between different things.

This diagram is called a network or **graph**. Once you have a graph, you don't even need the underlying map. The graph shows the important relationships in a simple way.

Graphs can represent just about any connection you want! For example, the vertices can represent individual students in your class, and the edges can show their friendships.

PUZZLE

Can you connect nine dots with four straight lines? Draw four straight lines that connect these nine dots without lifting your pencil from the paper. (See page 131 for the solution.)

Likewise, the vertices can represent individual websites, while the edges can show how they are connected on the Internet. In this way, lessons we learn about one network can apply to other, very different networks.

Euler discovered a simple way to prove the impossibility of crossing each of Königsberg's bridges only once on a single walk. His solution revolved around looking at each vertex and seeing how many edges were connected to it. For each vertex in the middle of the walk, Euler reasoned, edges connected to it will always come in pairs, with one edge representing your trip to the place and another symbolizing your trip away from it, as you continue your journey.

Therefore, vertices in the middle of your walk must have an even number of edges touching them, while only two vertices, one each at the beginning and end of your walk, can have an odd number of edges. Look at the graph of the bridges again.

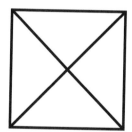

More than two vertices have an odd number of edges connected to them. This is a clear sign that a path crossing all of the bridges only once is impossible.

Here are other puzzles to try with this method. Can you draw a box with an X in the middle without lifting your pencil? What about this box with a roof on it? (See page 132 for the solution.)

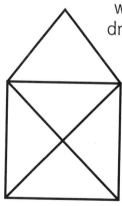

This diagram is a floor plan of a house with blank spaces showing the location of all its doors. Does a path exist that goes through each door only once? Hint: To draw a graph, place a vertex in each room and one outside the house. (see page 132 for the solution.)

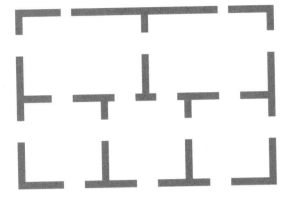

Six Degrees of Separation

The mathematics of graphs can be used to analyze networks of friends and acquaintances. For example, if you know 100 people, and each of these people knows 100 others, then you are connected to 10,000 people through your network of friends.

The pop culture idea of "six degrees of separation" is based on the belief that you are linked to everyone else in the world by six steps of connection or less. In other words, you know someone, who knows someone, who knows someone, who knows someone, who knows someone else who knows my uncle in Budapest, Hungary.

Random Walk ✹

HA! Scissors beat paper! Time to take a walk!

Oh, no! How close am I to the edge...

SPLASH

OKAY! BEST 3 out of 5?

At the lake by my house, children play a game on a raft. The game starts with two people in the middle of the raft, facing each other. They then play a game of rock-paper-scissors. The loser of the game has to take a step backward. The children continue playing rock-paper-scissors until someone backs up so far that they step off the raft and fall into the water.

ᗒᗒᗒᗒᗒᗒᗒᗒᗒᗒᗒᗒᗒᗒᗒᗒᗒ

You can play a solo version of this game right at home by flipping a coin. Determine where on the ground the ends of your "raft" lie, and then start flipping. If your coin shows "heads," take one step forward. If your coin shows "tails," take one step backward. Depending on the outcome of your flips, you may end up in the "water" sooner rather than later. It is more likely, however, that you will move back and forth for a while. Since your steps are random, this is called a **random walk**.

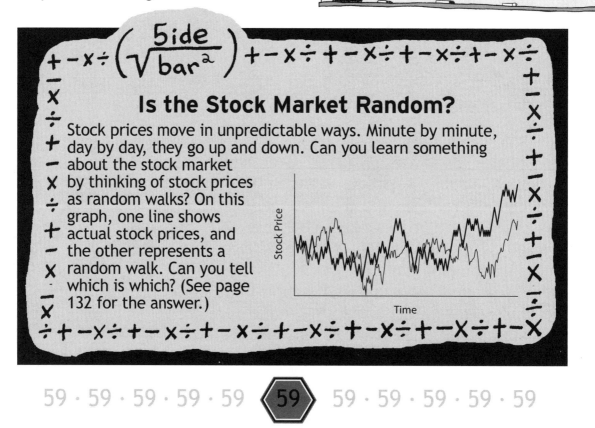

This may sound like fun and games, but to mathematicians it is serious business. Entire books are devoted to the properties of random walks. Random walks are important because many real-life systems behave like them. For example, molecules in a gas or liquid are knocked back and forth randomly by other molecules, so you can think of any one molecule as being on a random walk.

When molecules move randomly through a material, this process is called **diffusion**. You can see diffusion in action if you carefully place a drop of food coloring into a glass of water. At first, the color is concentrated in the place where you dropped the dye. Slowly, however, the dye spreads out until the entire glass of water is the same color. The molecules of dye are traveling in random walks.

WORDS + 2 + KNOW

random walk: a path whose steps are taken in random directions.

diffusion: mixing of molecules due to random movements.

Is the Stock Market Random?

Stock prices move in unpredictable ways. Minute by minute, day by day, they go up and down. Can you learn something about the stock market by thinking of stock prices as random walks? On this graph, one line shows actual stock prices, and the other represents a random walk. Can you tell which is which? (See page 132 for the answer.)

Stock Price

Time

Run a Random Ruler Race

Challenge your friends to the Random Ruler Race to see who can reach the end of a ruler first.

1 Each player places his or her nickel at the 6-inch (15-centimeter) mark on the ruler. All players flip their pennies at the same time.

2 Players whose pennies come up "heads" should move their nickels 1 inch (or 1 centimeter) to the right. Players whose pennies come up "tails" should move their nickels to the left.

3 Players should continue flipping coins until one player's nickel reaches either end of the ruler. That player is the winner.

Supplies

- 1 penny and 1 nickel for each player
- 12-inch (30-centimeter) ruler

Here is a graph of a sample game that shows the position of each player's nickel for every turn. Bob got lots of "tails" in a row and on the 5th turn was only 1 inch away from winning. Finally, on the 16th turn, Alice reached the end of the ruler and won the game.

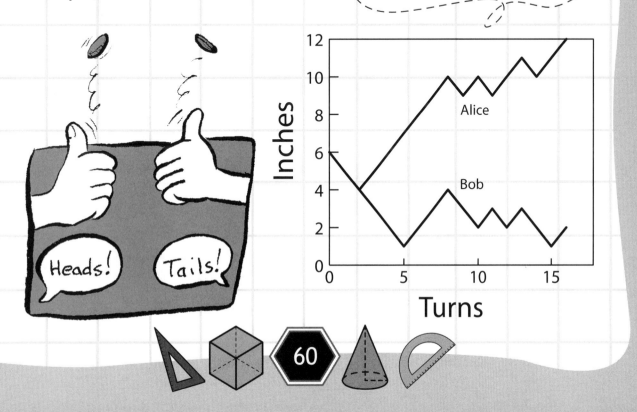

60

You may think that, because each step is random, you will not be able to predict many things about a random walk. True, no one can predict exactly where you will be at any point in your walk. However, you can use **probability** to learn some general properties.

> Heads again!

When you played the Random Ruler Race, were you surprised by how many coin tosses it took to reach one end of the ruler? The fastest possible way to win the race would have been with either six straight moves to the right or to the left. However, the probability of tossing six "heads" or "tails" in a row is only $1/32$. On a 30-centimeter metric ruler, the probability of tossing 15 "heads" or "tails" in a row, and achieving 15 straight moves in the same direction, is even less: $1/16384$.

WORDS + 2 + KNOW

probability: how likely it is, mathematically, that something will happen.

dimensions: different directions that you can measure. A line is a one-dimensional object because it can only be measured in terms of its length. A rectangle is a two-dimensional object because it can be measured in terms of its length and width. A cube is a three-dimensional object because it has length, width, and depth.

On the other hand, you might be wondering why you were ever able to finish the race. Shouldn't your coin come up "heads" and "tails" approximately the same number of times, so that your coin wiggles back and forth near the starting point and never really moves that far away? Surprisingly, in a one-**dimensional** random walk like this one, you are sure to reach any point you want, provided that your walk is long enough.

On average, it takes 36 coin tosses to reach the end of the 12-inch ruler (and 225 tosses to reach the end of the 30-centimeter ruler). How can you figure this out? Just square the distance you would like to move! To move 6 units from the starting point, for example, it will take an average of $6^2 = 36$ moves. For longer distances, the number of moves required to reach the end point gets much larger very quickly. For example, if you play this game on a 36-inch yardstick, you will need an average of $18^2 = 324$ moves to reach one of the two end points. How long would a random walk take to your friend's house? Should you pack a lunch or pack a suitcase?

Did you know?

In a one- and two-dimensional random walk, if you walk long enough, you will always make it back to your starting point. In three dimensions, however, you could wander around forever without ever returning home. In fact, in any three-dimensional random walk, you have only about a 34% chance of making it back to your starting point.

Try experimenting with random walks on a chessboard instead of a ruler. Now, your coin can move in four directions, instead of just two: left, right, forward, backward. Roll a die to determine which direction to move, assigning each direction a number from 1 to 4. If you roll a 5 or a 6, roll the die again. This scenario is an example of a two-dimensional random walk. Here is a graph of a two-dimensional random walk with 1,000 steps.

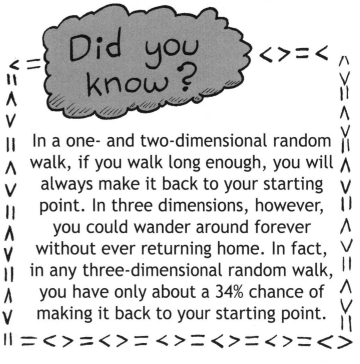

✷ Shortest Shoelace

What would you do if your shoelace broke during a basketball game? Fortunately, there are many different ways to lace your shoes. If you re-laced your shoe in a pattern that required a shorter length of lace, you might be able to retie your shoe with what you had left and then return to the game.

ooooooooooooooooooooo

There are an astounding number of ways to lace your shoes. With six pairs of eyelets you could lace your shoes so that the laces go across the shoe at each eyelet in 3,758,400 different patterns. With eight pairs of eyelets, there are 52,733,721,600 possible arrangements. Your options include messy lacings and neat ones, strong lacings and weak ones, and lacings that require very long or very short shoelaces.

Here are a few different ways to lace your shoes. Which pattern do you think uses the shortest shoelace? How can you tell? If you know how far apart the eyelets are from each other, both horizontally and vertically, you can calculate the length of the shoelace up to the top eyelets.

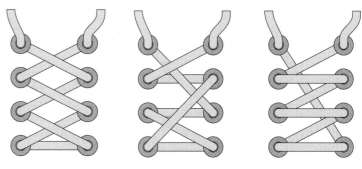

Let's assume that the eyelets on this shoe are 4 centimeters apart horizontally and 2 centimeters apart vertically. How long are the shoelaces? First, let's calculate the length of each segment of shoelace. For example, the first pattern is made up of 1 horizontal segment and 6 slanted ones. To figure out the length of the slanted segments, imagine a right triangle with the slanted segment as the hypotenuse, and then solve for the length of the hypotenuse using the Pythagorean theorem.

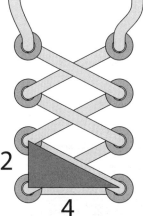

Once you've found the lengths of all the segments, add them together to find the total length of the shoelace. In the first pattern, the horizontal segment has a length of 4, and each of the slanted segments has a length of approximately 4.47. The total length of the shoelace in the first pattern, then, is 30.83 cm. What are the lengths of the shoelaces in the other two arrangements? Which pattern uses the shortest length of shoelace? (See page 132 for the solution.)

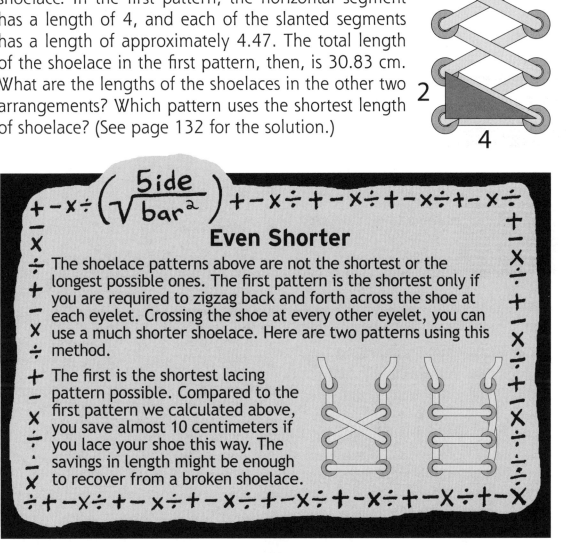

$$+-\times\div\left(\sqrt{\dfrac{\textbf{side}}{\textbf{bar}^2}}\right)+-\times\div+-\times\div+-\times\div+-\times\div$$

Even Shorter

The shoelace patterns above are not the shortest or the longest possible ones. The first pattern is the shortest only if you are required to zigzag back and forth across the shoe at each eyelet. Crossing the shoe at every other eyelet, you can use a much shorter shoelace. Here are two patterns using this method.

The first is the shortest lacing pattern possible. Compared to the first pattern we calculated above, you save almost 10 centimeters if you lace your shoe this way. The savings in length might be enough to recover from a broken shoelace.

Design the
Longest Shoelace Pattern

Up to this point, we've focused on the shortest possible shoelace patterns. Now, let's find the longest possible lacings for shoes with 8 and 10 eyelets.

1 Draw two columns of four dots each to represent eight eyelets.

2 Try to connect the dots with lines in a way that makes the longest possible path. Don't go through the same eyelet twice, and be creative! For example, you don't have to start at the bottom two eyelets or end at the top two.

3 Try different arrangements until you think you've found the best one. Repeat this process with 10 eyelets. (See page 132 for the solution.)

Supplies

- pencil • paper

Shapes

Look around you. What shapes do you see? Do you see triangles, squares, and circles? Math helps us define these basic shapes and describe their properties. In this section, we'll explore new ways to create these shapes and others like them. We'll fold some out of paper and draw others. You may already know how to find the area of a triangle and a circle, but we'll take a fresh look at these familiar formulas to see where they come from.

These simple shapes are the building blocks of more elaborate shapes, including three-dimensional ones like cubes and spheres. This section will introduce you to a family of solid shapes made up of triangles, squares, and pentagons. We'll also create exotic shapes with elegant curves that have the surprising property of being made entirely of straight lines. Maybe you will discover your new favorite shape.

✪ Polygons

From the simple rectangle of a picture frame to the complex shapes used in computer graphics, shapes are all around us. Mathematics provides us with ways to describe these shapes and learn about their properties.

ooooooooooooooooooooo

Polygons are shapes made out of line segments on a **plane** that are connected to enclose an area. They are named for how many sides they have. Polygons that have sides that are all the same length and angles that are all the same size are called **regular polygons**. They are the fundamental shapes in **geometry** and are used in many projects in this book.

WORDS + **2** + KNOW

polygon: a shape on a plane made up of line segments.

plane: a flat surface that extends forever.

regular polygon: a polygon with each side the same length and each angle the same size.

geometry: the study of shapes and their properties.

Many polygons with more than 10 sides have official names. However, you can also refer to them as n-gons, inserting the number of sides where n is. For example, a 13-sided shape is called a 13-gon.

Polygons

Sides	Name	Examples
3	triangle	
4	quadrilateral	
5	pentagon	
6	hexagon	
7	heptagon	
8	octagon	
9	nonagon	
10	decagon	

Form a Pentagon by Tying a Knot

Squares and equilateral triangles are much easier to draw than **regular pentagons**. It is difficult to estimate the exact angles that you need to draw in order to make a regular pentagon look right. In this activity, however, you will discover a simple way to create a regular pentagon by tying a knot in a strip of paper.

Supplies

- paper
- scissors

3 Continue folding over the ends until you are left with a regular pentagon.

1 Cut a long strip of paper about 1 inch (2 centimeters) wide. Tie a simple overhand knot in the paper (crisscross the two ends, tuck one end under, and pull).

2 Slowly and carefully pull the ends of the knot to tighten and flatten it. You want to end up with a tight knot that lies completely flat.

WORDS + 2 + KNOW

regular pentagon: a five-sided regular polygon.

vertex (of a polygon): a corner point.

radius: the distance from the center of a circle to any point on the circle.

Draw a Hexagon in a Circle

All regular polygons fit neatly inside a circle with each **vertex** touching the circle. The vertices divide the circle into arcs of equal lengths. You can use this fact to draw a regular polygon. For example, if you draw a circle and place a dot every 36 degrees around its outside edge, you will divide it into 10 sections. If you connect all of the dots using straight lines, you will create a regular decagon.

In this activity, you will draw a regular hexagon without measuring angles.

Supplies

- paper
- compass
- pencil
- ruler

1 Draw a circle with a compass. Hold the compass open the same distance that you used to create this circle for the rest of this activity.

2 Place the point of the compass on the outside edge of the circle, and make a mark on the circle where the other arm of the compass reaches.

3 Place the point of the compass on this mark, and repeat step 2. Continue around the circle.

4 Connect the marks on the circle with straight lines to create a regular hexagon.

To find out why this works, draw lines from the center of the circle to each of the hexagon's vertices. What do you see? The hexagon consists of six equilateral triangles. Two sides of each triangle lie along a **radius** of the circle. Since your compass was also set to the radius, it made the third side of each triangle the right length.

✿ Triangles

Triangles, the simplest polygons, have some very useful characteristics. Triangles often appear in structures that need to be very strong, like bridges and building frameworks. Why? Three beams connected in a triangle can form only one shape. In contrast, four beams connected in the rectangle can form more than one shape. If you put enough weight on one side of a rectangle, you can smash it into a **parallelogram.**

ooooooooooooooooooooo

Triangles are also important to understanding more complex polygons. If you know how to calculate side lengths, angles, and areas of triangles, you can figure out these values in other polygons.

Show the Angles in a Triangle Add Up to 180 degrees

A simple way to prove that the angles in a triangle always add up to 180 degrees is to cut a triangle out of paper, tear off its corners, and put the corners together so that the vertices of the triangle meet at a single point. Try this process with triangles of other shapes and sizes. No matter what triangle you start with, the corners will always add up to make a straight line (a 180-degree angle).

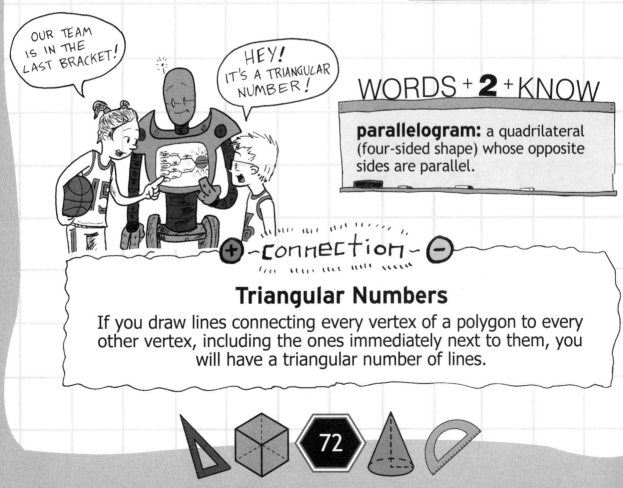

OUR TEAM IS IN THE LAST BRACKET!

HEY! IT'S A TRIANGULAR NUMBER!

WORDS + **2** + KNOW

parallelogram: a quadrilateral (four-sided shape) whose opposite sides are parallel.

-connection-

Triangular Numbers

If you draw lines connecting every vertex of a polygon to every other vertex, including the ones immediately next to them, you will have a triangular number of lines.

Show the Triangle Area Formula

In this activity, you'll be able to see why the area of a triangle is one-half the length of the base times the height. We'll use the same method as the one we used with penny triangles: we'll calculate the area of two triangles, and then cut the value in half.

1 Cut out two identical triangles. Draw a dashed line showing the height of one triangle. Label the base on the other triangle.

2 Turn one triangle upside down and place the two triangles together to make a parallelogram. Cut off the tip of the parallelogram at the dashed line.

3 Move the piece you just cut off to the other side of the parallelogram to form a rectangle.

4 Calculate the area of the rectangle. The area is the length (the base of the triangle) times the width (the height of the triangle). Since this is the area of two triangles, divide it in half to find the area of one: one-half of the base times the height.

Supplies

- paper
- scissors
- pencil

73

Stars ✪

Stars are a popular symbol in our culture, often used to represent quality. For example, you may rate your favorite movie by giving it five stars. Likewise, the more stars that army generals have, the higher their rank. Stars appear on flags, company logos, and police officers' badges. In this section, we'll explore this shape and see how it relates to other ideas in math.

Did you know?

If you cut an apple in half right across the core, the seeds form a five-pointed star.

Draw a Star Polygon

more on the Web

You can make a star by connecting the vertices of a regular polygon. For example, if you connect every other vertex of this regular pentagon (five-sided polygon), you will make a five-pointed star. A star made this way is called a **star polygon**. You can also create stars with more than five points using this method. Try making a seven-pointed star polygon inside this heptagon (seven-sided polygon).

Did you connect every other vertex? Try it again, this time connecting every third vertex. You will create a different seven-pointed star. If you connect every third vertex of the pentagon above, however, you will produce the same star as connecting every other vertex. Try it, and see if you can figure out why.

In some cases, connecting the vertices of a polygon will not produce a star polygon. For example, if you connect every other vertex of a hexagon (six-sided polygon), you will return to your starting point having formed only a triangle. Three vertices of the hexagon will remain unconnected. You can still make a star, however, if you continue connecting vertices starting with the next available vertex. This activity shows that a six-pointed star is really just two overlapping triangles. Can you make a star out of two overlapping squares? How about three overlapping squares? What regular polygons should you use to create these stars?

WORDS + 2 + KNOW

star polygon: a star formed by connecting every other (or every third, fourth, etc.) vertex of a regular polygon.

75

Fold and Cut a Star

more on the Web If you fold a piece of paper just right, you can cut out a five-pointed star with only one cut!

Supplies

- sheet of paper, 8½ by 11 inches
- scissors • ruler

1 Cut 1 inch (2.5 centimeters) off the bottom of the sheet of paper to make it 8½ by 10 inches (21.6 by 25.4 centimeters).

2 Fold the sheet in half. Fold it in half again, make a crease, and open it.

3 Fold so that the top right corner touches the middle of the left edge.

4 Fold the top left corner flap down. Fold the flap over again. Cut along the dashed line. Open it up to see your star.

To make the star look prettier, push all the long folds up and pull all the short folds down.

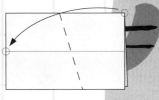

$$+-\times\div\left(\sqrt{\frac{5ide}{bar^2}}\right)+-\times\div+-\times\div+-\times\div+-\times\div$$

Polygons Inside Star Polygons

There is a pentagon in the center of every five-pointed star polygon. In fact, in the center of every star polygon, there is a smaller version of the regular polygon used to create it. This fact leads to another method of creating star polygons. Start with a regular polygon and extend the lines forming the sides of the polygons until they meet.

$\cdot\times\div+-\times\div+-\times\div+-\times\div+-\times\div+-\times$

✪ Circles

> The circle is the perfect, first, most beautiful form.

Aristotle, an ancient Greek philosopher, called the circle "the perfect, first, most beautiful form." It is not hard to see why. The circle is a simple and highly **symmetrical** shape.

The Circumference of the Earth

In addition to developing his method for finding prime numbers, Eratosthenes also calculated the **circumference** of the earth using the angle of the sun overhead in two different cities. He knew that in Syene, the sun was straight overhead on the longest day of the year. About 500 miles (800 kilometers) away in Alexandria, where he lived, the sun was 7.2 degrees lower in the sky (or, as he put it, "one fiftieth of a circle"). Using this information, he calculated the circumference of the earth, coming very close to its actual value—a remarkable feat for the time. Not only did he believe that the earth was round in the year 250 BCE, he had a good sense of just how big it was.

Despite the circle's apparent simplicity, it puzzled mathematicians for thousands of years as they struggled to find its circumference and area. A circle 1 foot in **diameter** has a circumference of slightly more than 3 feet. Its circumference is equal to π (written as the Greek letter and pronounced "pie") feet, to be exact. Calculating the value of π is not an easy task.

Ancient mathematicians narrowed in on the value of π by calculating the perimeters of regular polygons with many sides. The more sides they used for their polygons, the closer the shapes came to a circle, and thus the better their perimeters approximated that of a circle. If you look at the polygons on page 68, for example, you will see that even a decagon (a 10-sided polygon) somewhat resembles a circle. Imagine, then, how much more closely a 1000-gon resembles a circle.

WORDS ＋**2**＋KNOW

symmetrical: a property of a shape that looks the same if you rotate it or look at it in a mirror.

circumference: the distance around a circle.

diameter: a straight line running from one side of a circle to the other through the center.

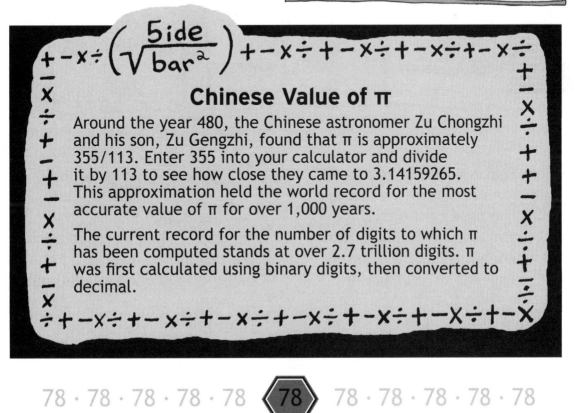

Chinese Value of π

Around the year 480, the Chinese astronomer Zu Chongzhi and his son, Zu Gengzhi, found that π is approximately 355/113. Enter 355 into your calculator and divide it by 113 to see how close they came to 3.14159265. This approximation held the world record for the most accurate value of π for over 1,000 years.

The current record for the number of digits to which π has been computed stands at over 2.7 trillion digits. π was first calculated using binary digits, then converted to decimal.

Show the Area of a Circle

This activity will show that the area of a circle is π times the radius squared or πr^2.

1 Wind the yarn into a flat spiral. Place a piece of tape onto the yarn from the middle of the spiral to the edge.

2 Cut the yarn next to the tape. Unwind the yarn to form a right triangle.

3 Calculate the area of the triangle using the equation A= ½ bh where b is the length of the base and h is the height of the triangle.

Notice that the height of the triangle is the radius of the circle and that the base of the triangle is the circumference of the circle (2 × π × radius). Half of the base, then, is π × radius. Put these expressions into the triangle area formula and you will get the circle area formula $A = \pi r^2$.

Did you know?

If you want a fence to enclose the largest area, arrange it in the shape of a circle. You will get 27% more area inside a circular fence than you will with a square fence of the same length.

Möbius Strip ✵

A strip of paper connected into a loop with a half twist is one of the most intriguing shapes that you may ever encounter. For such a seemingly simple shape, it has some amazing qualities.

○○○○○○○○○○○○○○○○○○○○

A sheet of paper has two sides. An ant crawling on one side of the paper couldn't get to the other side without crossing an edge. A Möbius strip, in contrast, is one-sided. In other words, an ant could walk from any point on the surface to any other point without ever crossing an edge. If you try coloring a Möbius strip with crayons, you will see that you can't color one side blue and the other side green because there is only one side.

We found that to shade any map on a plane so that no two bordering regions are the same color, it takes four colors (see page 54). On a Möbius strip, it takes six colors. Challenge yourself by drawing a six-color map on a Möbius strip made from an overhead transparency sheet. Making the strip transparent is like using a strip with zero thickness.

Marvel at a Möbius Strip

In this activity you will create your own Möbius strip, then explore some of its amazing qualities.

1 Cut a long strip of newspaper about 2 inches (5 centimeters) wide.

2 Bring the ends of the strip together to form a loop. Before you tape the ends together, give one end of the paper a half-twist.

3 Now tape the ends together to form your Möbius strip.

Supplies

- newspaper
- scissors
- tape
- pencil

Joke

Q: Why did the chicken cross the Möbius strip?

A: To get to the same side.

Activity 1:

First, place your pencil in the middle of your Möbius strip and draw a line along the length of the strip, keeping your pencil on the paper the whole time.

What happened? Your pencil line is on both sides of the paper. How did you accomplish this without your pencil ever going over an edge? A Möbius strip really does have only one side.

Activity 2:

Now cut the Möbius strip along the line you just drew. Does the strip fall into two pieces? No? Welcome to the wacky world of the Möbius strip!

Cut the strip down the middle again. Another surprise!

Activity 3:

Cut a Möbius strip along a line one-third of the way from the edge of the strip.

Make more Möbius strips, experimenting with different numbers of twists: a half twist, a whole twist, 1½ twists, and so on. What happens when you cut them? Is there a pattern?

✺ Platonic Solids

There is something special about the five **solids** shown here that sets them apart from other **polyhedra**. For example, look at the dodecahedron, the second shape from the right, above. It is made up of 12 regular pentagons, so each **face** is the same. Moreover, each vertex has the same number of pentagons meeting there.

○○○○○○○○○○○○○○○○○○

The other four solids shown here also have regular polygon faces and the same number of faces at each vertex. These five solids are called **Platonic solids** after Plato, the ancient Greek philosopher who studied them.

Wouldn't these solids make great dice? They certainly are symmetrical enough.

WORDS + **2** + KNOW

solid: a three-dimensional geometric shape.

polyhedra: The plural of polyhedron, which is a solid formed with polygons as faces.

face: a flat surface on a solid.

Platonic solids: the five solids made up of regular polygons with the same number of faces meeting at each vertex. The Platonic solids are the tetrahedron, cube, octahedron, dodecahedron, and icosahedron.

Grow Your Own Crystals

Some minerals form crystals in the shape of Platonic solids. A crystal of tetrahedrite looks like a tetrahedron. A diamond naturally forms octahedral crystals. In this activity, you can grow your own crystals to see what shapes they make.

1 With an adult's help, bring 1 cup of water to a boil in the pot.

2 Take the pot off the stove and stir in some salt. Dissolve as much salt as you possibly can in the water.

3 After the salt water cools, pour it into the glass jar.

4 Tie a paper clip on one end of the string. Tie the other end of the string around the middle of the pencil, so that when you place the pencil over the jar, the paper clip hangs into the solution and almost touches the bottom. After a few days, crystals should form on the paper clip. Look at them through a magnifying glass to see their shape.

Supplies

- pot
- 1 cup of water
- stove
- salt
- spoon
- small glass jar
- string
- paper clip
- pencil
- magnifying glass

Make Platonic Solids

Why are there only five Platonic solids? Shouldn't there be more? For example, why isn't there a Platonic solid with hexagonal faces? In this activity, you will construct the five Platonic solids, and discover why only that many exist.

more on the Web

Tetrahedron
a solid with 4 triangular faces
3 polygons meet at each vertex
4 big triangles

Cube
a solid with 6 square faces
3 polygons meet at each vertex
6 squares

Octahedron
a solid with 8 triangular faces
4 polygons meet at each vertex
8 small triangles

Dodecahedron
a solid with12 pentagonal faces
3 polygons meet at each vertex
12 pentagons

Icosahedron
a solid with 20 triangular faces
5 polygons meet at each vertex
20 small triangles

Supplies

- paper or card stock
- scissors
- tape

1 Photocopy and cut out the polygons in the template. Check at the left to see how many polygons you will need for each Platonic solid.

2 Tape the polygons together so that the right number of faces meets at each vertex. For prettier models, tape the pieces together on the insides of the models.

3 Once you have made all the models, you may have a better idea why more Platonic solids don't exist. To make the tetrahedron, octahedron, and icosahedron, you taped three, four, and five triangles together at one vertex. The next option is to tape six equilateral triangles at each vertex. Cut out six more triangles and try it. What happens? When taped together, the six triangles just lie flat on the table. You can't make a solid out of them. The same is true of four squares and three hexagons. No matter how hard you try, you won't be able to find other combinations of regular polygons that form a Platonic solid.

Although there are only five Platonic solids in total, there are many other solids built with different combinations of regular polygons. While not as symmetrical, they are equally beautiful.

See How Platonic Solids are Related

Certain Platonic solids are closely related to each other. For example, the octahedron and cube are both capable of fitting snugly inside each other, with each vertex of one solid touching the middle of the face of the other. For this reason, they are called duals of each other. The dodecahedron and the icosahedron are also duals. The poor tetrahedron stands alone: it is the dual of itself.

1 Using the directions from the previous activity, make a tetrahedron, an octahedron, and a cube. Tape only one edge of the top of the cube, so that the top can be opened like a lid.

2 Place the octahedron inside the cube so that each vertex of the octahedron touches a face of the cube. This arrangement demonstrates that the cube and the octahedron are duals. The relationship is reciprocal: if you made a bigger octahedron, the cube would fit inside it the same way.

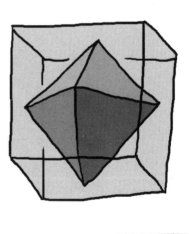

3 Remove the octahedron and place the tetrahedron inside the cube. At first, it seems like the tetrahedron is too large to fit inside, but if you position it correctly, it will slide into place. Notice that the tetrahedron shares four vertices with the cube. Until you try this, it is hard to visualize how this could possibly be the case.

Tetrahedron ✹

UGH! WHO CUT THE TETRAHEDRON?

The simplest Platonic solid is the tetrahedron, made out of four equilateral triangles. Tetrahedra are all around us, although most are too small to see.

ooooooooooooooooooo

The atoms in molecules, for example, sometimes arrange themselves into the shape of a tetrahedron. Methane, one of the gases in farts, has a tetrahedral structure. A carbon atom sits in the center of the tetrahedron, and is attached to 4 hydrogen atoms. The hydrogen atoms repel each other, so they retreat to the vertices of a tetrahedron to be as far apart from each other as they can.

A tetrahedron, like the triangles that form it, is a very rigid shape. This is why tripods are so stable. A frame made in the shape of a cube can be deformed much more easily than one made in the shape of a tetrahedron. The carbon atoms in diamonds, which are among the hardest materials in the world, are connected in a tetrahedral arrangement.

PUZZLE

For all its advantages in terms of strength, the tetrahedron rarely occurs in architecture, except as part of a framework to hold up a large roof. Even then, it needs a partner shape to work best. You can't stack tetrahedra together to fill space, because they just don't fit together nicely. They need to be combined with octahedra. Make a few tetrahedra and octahedra to see how they fit together.

Create a Tetrahedron from an Envelope

One easy and surprising way to make a tetrahedron is to quickly fold one from an envelope.

1 Cut a 3½-inch (9-centimeter) section off the end of the envelope. For other envelope sizes, cut a section that is 0.87 times as long as the envelope is wide.

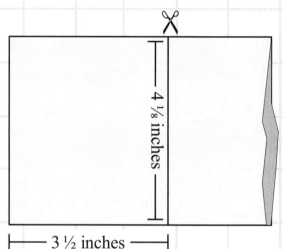

4 ⅛ inches

3 ½ inches

2 Fold the end that you just cut in half and make a short crease to mark the middle of the open side.

3 Make a fold that goes from each corner to the middle mark. Fold these creases back and forth.

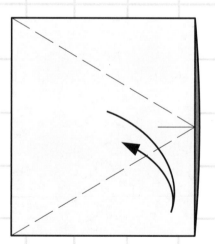

4 Open the envelope wider and wider until the edges meet again. Tape the edges together.

Supplies

- sealed, U.S. standard business envelope
- ruler
- scissors
- tape

Make a Tetrahedral Puzzle

Ready to challenge yourself? In this activity, you'll create a puzzle that's surprisingly difficult, considering that it has only two pieces.

1 Photocopy and cut out two copies of the template from card stock.

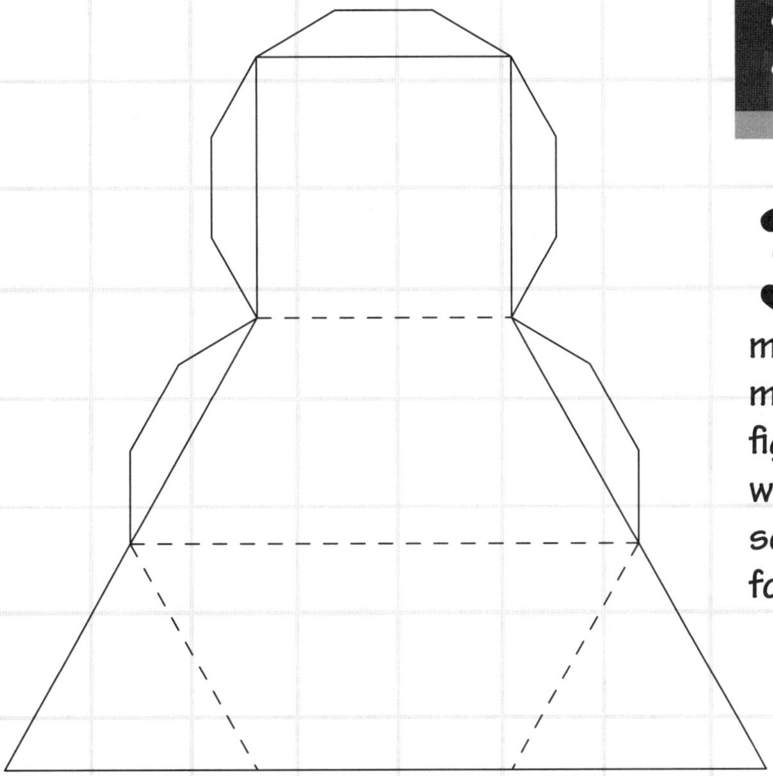

Supplies

- card stock
- scissors
- glue

3 Assemble the two pieces to form a tetrahedron. You may struggle for a few minutes, but once you figure it out, you will wonder why it took you so long! (See page 132 for the solution.)

2 Fold along the dashed lines and glue each piece together at the tabs.

Fly a Tetrahedral Kite

more on the Web

Alexander Graham Bell worked on many other inventions after he invented the telephone. Bell believed that if he could invent a kite that was strong, light, and flew very well, he could use its design to make the first airplane. He eventually created an enormous kite consisting of 3,393 small tetrahedra that was capable of carrying a person 168 feet (51 meters) into the air as it was towed behind a steamship. Meanwhile, the Wright brothers made their historic first flight at Kitty Hawk.

1 Cut a piece of string 40 inches (1 meter) long and another piece 30 inches (75 centimeters) long. Slip both strings through a straw together.

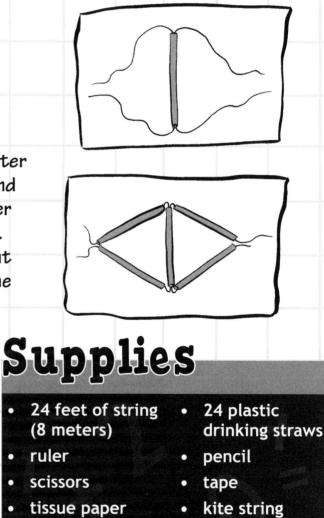

2 Slip each end of the shorter string through straws and tie the two ends together to create a triangle of straws. The triangle should be taut, but not so tight that it buckles the straws. Don't trim the extra string yet.

3 Slip each end of the longer string through straws. Gather most of the extra string on one side, and then tie a knot, reserving this extra string.

Supplies

- 24 feet of string (8 meters)
- ruler
- scissors
- tissue paper
- 24 plastic drinking straws
- pencil
- tape
- kite string

91

4 Slip a straw over the extra string from step 3. Tie the free end of the string to the extra string at the top of the first triangle of straws in order to form a tetrahedron.

5 Trace the outline of two straw triangles onto tissue paper. Draw tabs that extend about an inch (2 centimeters) past the straws. Cut out the shape. Cover two faces of the tetrahedron with the tissue paper and tape it into place.

6 Repeating steps 1 through 5, make three more tetrahedra.

7 Tie the four tetrahedra together at their corners to form a larger tetrahedron.

8 Tie a small loop in the middle of a 2-foot-long (60-centimeter) piece of string and tie the ends of the string to the top and bottom of the topmost tetrahedron.

9 Tie your kite string to this loop and fly it in a steady wind.

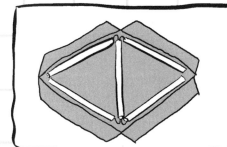

When you stack four tetrahedra to make the kite, notice that they alone don't fit together to fill space. The gap in the middle of the kite is an octahedron.

✿ Icosahedron

PRESENTING: the icosahedron!

Three of the five Platonic solids are made up of equilateral triangles. The most elaborate is the icosahedron with 20 faces. Every icosahedron is made of three interlocking golden rectangles.

"It is certain." What did you ask?

"Is your shape a icosahedron?"

Did you know?

The Magic 8-Ball® toy contains an icosahedron with answers printed on each of its faces. The face that floats to the top shows up in the clear window.

more on the Web

Make Icosahedral Decorations

Here is a fun way to make decorations based on an icosahedron.

1 Use a compass to draw 20 circles on colored paper. Cut them out. You can save time by folding the paper in half and cutting out two circles at a time.

2 Fold a circle so that any point on the edge touches the center.

3 Fold the circle two more times to make an equilateral triangle.

4 Use this triangle as a guide to fold tabs on the other circles. Partially open the tabs.

5 Glue five triangles together at the tabs to make a "hat." Make a second hat.

6 Make a "belt" out of 10 triangles in a row alternately pointing up and down. Glue the belt into a loop. Glue the two hats onto the belt to finish your decoration.

Supplies

- compass
- colored paper
- scissors
- glue

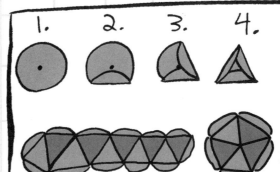

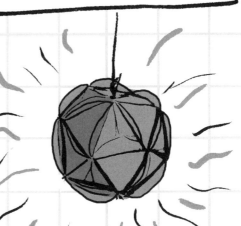

Build an Icosahedron from Golden Rectangles

more on the Web

Supplies

- boxboard
- scissors
- craft knife
- craft thread

Use golden rectangles to construct an icosahedron.

1 Photocopy and cut out three rectangles from boxboard using the template.

2 Use a craft knife to cut the vertical center slot on all three rectangles. Cut the horizontal side slot on only one rectangle. Make the slots wide enough so that the other pieces easily slide into them.

3 Cut a short slit in each corner of the rectangles. Fit the three rectangles together. Challenge yourself by trying to figure out how to do this alone. If you do need more detailed instructions, however, see page 132.

4 Slip the craft thread into the slits to connect each corner to its nearest neighbors.

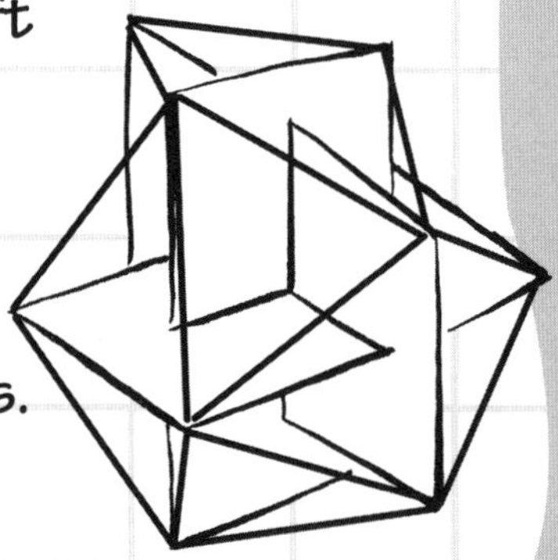

(cut this slot on only one rectangle)

Pyramids ✪

You don't have to travel to Egypt to see a **pyramid**. For example, church steeples often take the shape of a pyramid, with triangular roof sections meeting each other at one point. Any polygon can form the **base** of a pyramid. Tetrahedra, one type of pyramid, have a triangular base. The pyramids of Egypt have a square base, while quartz crystals have a hexagonal base.

WORDS + 2 + KNOW

pyramid: a solid with a polygon for a base and triangles that meet at a point for all the other faces.

base (of a pyramid): the bottom face of a pyramid, the one that doesn't meet at the point where the other faces meet.

volume: the amount of space an object takes up.

Discover the Volume of a Pyramid

more on the Web

How much rice does a pyramid hold compared to a cube with the same base and height? Half the **volume**? One third? Even less? In this activity, we'll construct a cube and a pyramid to find out.

1 Photocopy and cut out the templates from card stock. Fold them along the dashed lines. Tape the tabs to make an open pyramid and cube.

2 Place the pyramid inside the cube. Notice that the pyramid and the cube have bases with the same area, and they are both the same height.

3 Completely fill the pyramid with rice and empty it into the cube. Count how many times you have to do this to fill the cube.

Supplies

- card stock
- scissors
- tape
- uncooked rice

97

Geodesic Domes ✸

Platonic solids are simple and beautiful. It is difficult to imagine any shapes that could improve on them. About one hundred years ago, however, an engineer named Walther Bauersfeld designed a new type of dome to hold the first modern planetarium. The architect R. Buckminster Fuller later reinvented, refined, and popularized the dome.

ooooooooooooooooooooo

A **geodesic dome** begins as a Platonic solid, often an icosahedron. Each face is then split into smaller triangles, whose vertices are shifted outward to make it more **spherical**.

WORDS + **2** + KNOW

geodesic dome: a dome built out of triangles to approximate a part of a sphere.

spherical: shaped round, like a sphere.

Make a Geodesic Dome Big Enough to Sit In

more on the Web

Simple domes split each triangular face into 4 smaller triangles. Elaborate domes have 9, 16, 25, or even 36 smaller triangles for every face of the underlying icosahedron. Unlike a Platonic solid, though, a geodesic dome has edges that are not all the same length.

In this activity, you'll build a geodesic dome large enough for you to sit in. You might want to ask some friends or classmates for help, because this model requires making many parts.

1 Spread out a full sheet of newspaper on a flat surface. Moving from the bottom right corner to the top left corner, roll the newspaper up as tightly as possible, and then tape it. The more tightly you roll the newspaper, the stronger the dome will be. For this reason, it may be helpful to roll the newspaper around a bamboo skewer for the first few turns, before removing the skewer and continuing without it.

2 Create 65 of these newspaper rolls. The rolls will serve as struts, or supports, of the geodesic dome.

Supplies

- lots of newspaper
- bamboo skewer (optional)
- masking tape
- ruler
- scissors

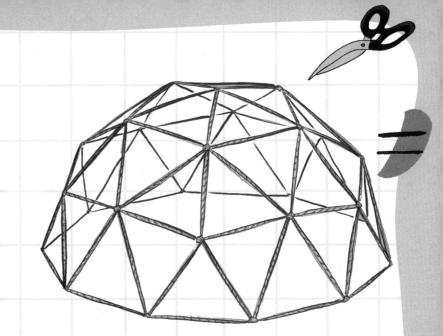

3 Cut 35 of the struts to be 21 inches long (50 centimeters) and 30 struts to be 18½ inches long (44 centimeters).

4 Place 10 long struts on the floor in the shape of a decagon. Place 2 long and 2 short struts in alternating pairs around the inside of the decagon, as shown. Tape the ends of all the struts together with masking tape.

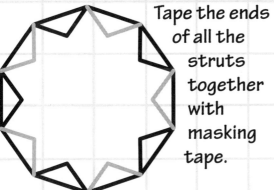

long strut ——
short strut ——

5 Tape 10 short struts in place around the inside of the dome. This will start raising its walls. The structure will remain floppy, however, until the last strut is in place. Continue adding struts as shown in the diagram.

Note that the diagrams are not to scale, but do show the placements of struts.

✪ Hyperboloid

Think of a circle mounted on a stick like a lollipop. If you spin the stick, the circle forms the shape of a sphere. Do the same with an ellipse, and you create an ellipsoid, a shape that looks like a stretched-out sphere.

ooooooooooooooooooooo

If you rotate a parabola or a hyperbola, you don't produce a solid shape, but rather a surface. Spin a parabola, and you create a dish-shaped paraboloid. Depending on how you rotate a hyperbola, you can produce two different surfaces. Spinning a hyperbola one way makes two separate bowl-shaped parts, and spinning it the other way produces a single curved surface. In this section, we'll explore the properties of the second type of hyperboloid, called the **hyperboloid of one sheet**.

You may have already seen a hyperboloid before. Cooling towers for nuclear power plants are made in this shape because it allows builders to make the tower walls much thinner than those of a cylindrical tower. In fact, if a hyperboloid cooling tower were shrunk to the size of an egg, its walls would be thinner than an eggshell.

Amazingly, although a hyperboloid has graceful curves, you can construct one using only straight lines.

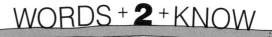

WORDS + 2 + KNOW

ellipsoid: a solid with elliptical cross sections.

hyperboloid of one sheet: a surface formed by rotating a hyperbola.

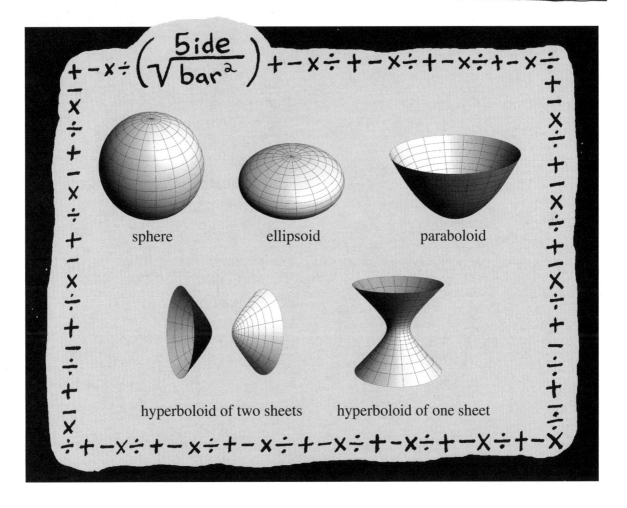

sphere ellipsoid paraboloid

hyperboloid of two sheets hyperboloid of one sheet

Make a Hyperboloid

more on the Web

We'll create a hyperboloid out of string to see how it can be made using only straight lines.

1 Cut two strips of paper 4 inches wide (10 centimeters) and tape them together to make one long strip of paper.

2 Wrap the strip of paper around the straight section of the bottle, and cut it so that it is just long enough to fit.

3 Fold the strip in half four times to make creases that divide it into 16ths.

Supplies

- paper
- scissors
- empty 2-liter plastic soda bottle
- tape
- pushpin
- pencil
- craft thread

4 Unfold the strip, wrap it around the bottle, and tape it in place.

5 With a pushpin, poke a hole in the bottle at the top and bottom of each crease to produce 2 rings of 16 holes each. Remove the paper strip. Use the tip of the pencil to enlarge each hole.

6 Cut off the top and bottom of the bottle about ½ inch (1 centimeter) above the top ring and ½ inch (1 centimeter) below the bottom ring of holes.

7 Insert the thread through a hole in the bottom ring of holes. Pull the thread out through a hole in the top ring of holes about five holes to the left of the bottom hole that you started with.

8 Insert the thread back into the cylinder through the next hole to the left in the top ring of holes. Pull the thread out the next hole to the left in the bottom ring of holes.

9 Continue around the cylinder until you reach the hole you started with. Pull the string taut and tie the beginning and the end together.

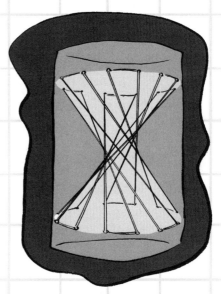

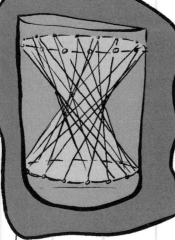

The shape you just formed is a hyperboloid of one sheet. Notice that even though the hyperboloid is curved, each string that makes it up is straight. You can make your model even more beautiful by threading the holes with another color of string slanting in the opposite direction. The two strings will form a crisscross pattern on the surface.

Surfaces made up of straight lines, like this one, are called ruled surfaces, where "ruled" refers to straight lines, as in the word ruler. Other ruled surfaces include planes, cylinders, and cones. Hyperboloids take this concept one step further. Since they can be made of two sets of lines slanting in different directions, they are doubly ruled surfaces.

Pass a Straight Line

For many people, the fact that straight lines are able to produce a curved surface is very surprising. In this activity, you can take advantage of this fact to astound your friends by showing them how you can pass a straight line through a curved slot in a piece of paper.

1 Photocopy and cut out the template on page 107 from card stock. Cut one straw 5 inches (13 centimeters) long.

2 Poke a hole through the middle of the two straws with a pushpin.

3 Push the bamboo skewer through both holes and position the 2 straws 1¼ inches (3 centimeters) apart on the skewer.

4 Cut off the extra lengths of bamboo skewer on both sides.

Supplies

- card stock
- scissors
- 2 drinking straws
- pushpin
- bamboo skewer (or sturdy round toothpick)
- tape

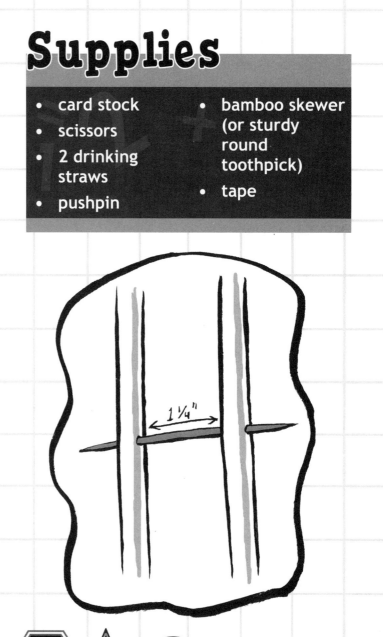

1 ¼"

Through a Curved Slot

5 Place the long straw on the tabs of the card stock piece so that the bamboo skewer lines up with the horizontal slot.

6 Curl the tabs around the straw and tape them to the card stock so that the short straw can spin freely.

7 Twist the short straw so that it is no longer parallel to the long straw, but is slanted 45 degrees.

8 Spin the long straw so that the short straw passes through the curved slot. You may have to adjust the distance between the straws and the angle of the short straw to keep it from hitting the sides of the slot.

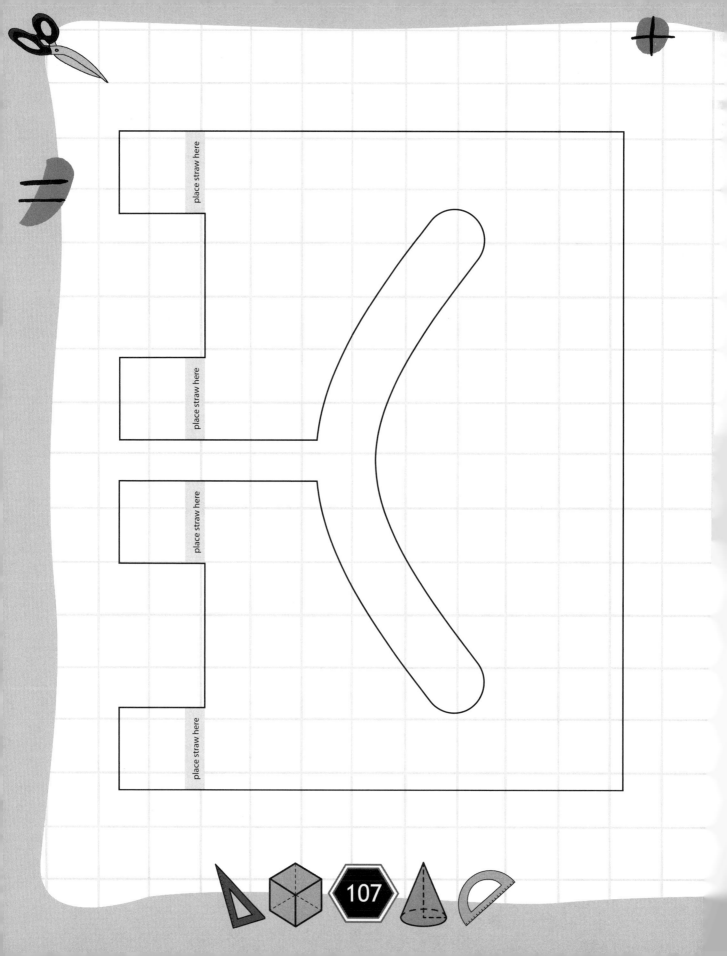

place straw here

place straw here

place straw here

place straw here

107

Hyperbolic Paraboloid ✜

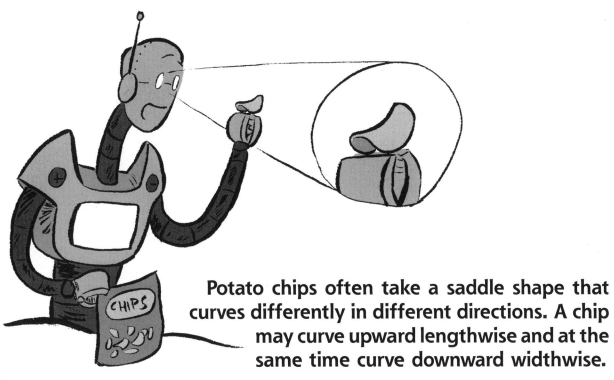

Potato chips often take a saddle shape that curves differently in different directions. A chip may curve upward lengthwise and at the same time curve downward widthwise.

ooooooooooooooooo

Now imagine an ideal potato chip with curves that are parabolas. This potato chip has the shape of a **hyperbolic paraboloid**. If you cut this shape vertically, you will see a parabolic cross section. Likewise, if you cut it horizontally, you will find a hyperbola. A hyperbolic paraboloid, then, combines these two conic sections in one amazing surface. Sports arenas, airport terminals, and even restaurants have been built with roofs in the shape of hyperbolic paraboloids.

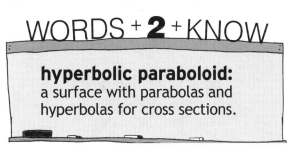

WORDS + **2** + KNOW

hyperbolic paraboloid: a surface with parabolas and hyperbolas for cross sections.

Make a Hyperbolic Paraboloid

more on the Web

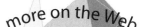

Like the hyperboloid, the hyperbolic paraboloid is a doubly ruled surface, which means that it can be built from only straight lines.

1 Photocopy and cut out the square and rectangle templates from boxboard. Cut short slits around the square at the marks.

2 Fold along the dotted line and cut the long slit in the middle of the square. Partially open the square again to make a 90-degree angle.

3 Slip the rectangle into the slit in the square to form a base. You may need to cut the slit a little wider to allow the rectangle to fit.

4 Tape the end of the craft thread to the underside of the square near slit number 1. Pull the thread up through slit 1 and down slit 2. Bring the thread up slit 3 and down slit 4 and so on.

5 Using a different color thread, repeat the process on the other pair of sides.

Supplies

- boxboard
- scissors
- craft thread or string
- tape

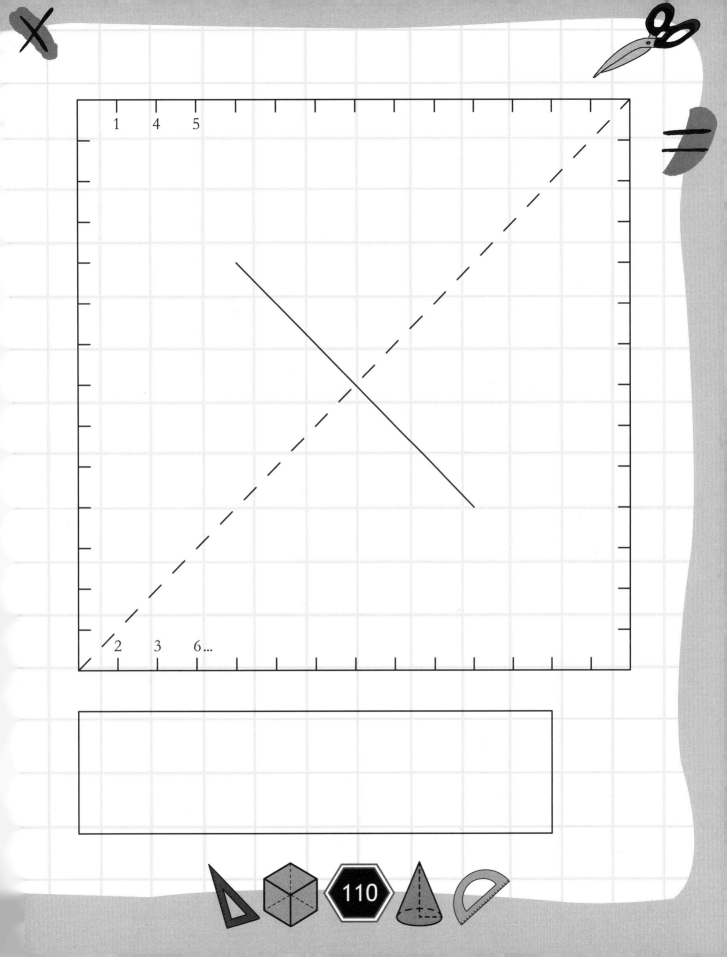

1   4   5

2   3   6...

110

Patterns

Throughout this book we've witnessed the beauty of math. We've created the graceful curve of a parabola, the pleasing symmetry of a dodecahedron, and the elegant form of a hyperboloid. We've seen examples in nature and architecture of striking shapes that exhibit mathematical beauty.

○○○○○○○○○○○○○○○○○○○○○○

In this section, we'll focus on the artistic side of math by making patterns, shapes, and designs. We will create parabolas out of string art, tile designs out of polygons, and drawings on cones. We'll look at patterns in bubbles and snowflakes and see how simple rules create surprisingly complex patterns.

String Art ✹

Placed according to simple rules, a series of straight lines can create beautiful curves. You'll craft incredible string art based on a parabola. With different string patterns, you can make other shapes as well. There are heart-shaped curves, called cardioids, and kidney-shaped curves, called nephroids.

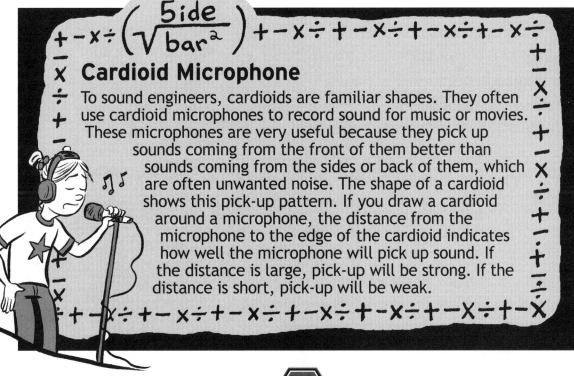

$+ - × ÷ \left(\sqrt{\dfrac{5ide}{bar^2}} \right) + - × ÷ + - × ÷ + - × ÷ + - × ÷$

Cardioid Microphone

To sound engineers, cardioids are familiar shapes. They often use cardioid microphones to record sound for music or movies. These microphones are very useful because they pick up sounds coming from the front of them better than sounds coming from the sides or back of them, which are often unwanted noise. The shape of a cardioid shows this pick-up pattern. If you draw a cardioid around a microphone, the distance from the microphone to the edge of the cardioid indicates how well the microphone will pick up sound. If the distance is large, pick-up will be strong. If the distance is short, pick-up will be weak.

Make String Art in a Circle

more on the Web

In this activity, you will connect points around a circle to make a heart-shaped curve known as a cardioid.

1 Photocopy and cut out the template from boxboard. Cut short slits around the circumference of the circle where marked.

2 Tape the end of the thread to the back of the circle.

3 Slip the thread up through slit number 1 and down through slit number 2. Slip the thread up through slit number 4 and down through slit number 2.

4 Continue connecting slits in the following pattern: up through slit 3, down through slit 6, up 8, down 4, up 5, down 10, and so on. In other words, always connect one number to another number that is twice as large. To avoid having lots of extra thread on the back of the circle, however, switch the direction of the thread every other time.

Supplies

- boxboard
- scissors
- craft thread
- tape

5 Here's what to do when you reach the large numbers. For example, according to the instructions, you should connect slit 36 to slit 72, but there is no slit 72! Since we are going around a circle, think of the numbers as starting all over again after slit 71, so the 72nd slit around the circle is actually the same as slit 0. Likewise, the 73rd slit around is the same as slit 1, and so on.

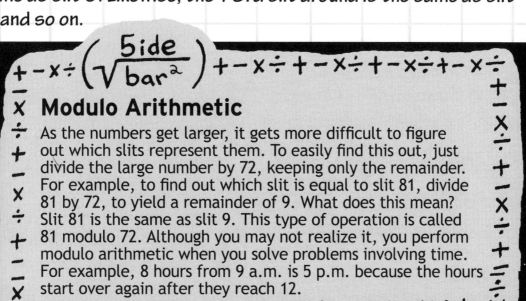

Modulo Arithmetic

As the numbers get larger, it gets more difficult to figure out which slits represent them. To easily find this out, just divide the large number by 72, keeping only the remainder. For example, to find out which slit is equal to slit 81, divide 81 by 72, to yield a remainder of 9. What does this mean? Slit 81 is the same as slit 9. This type of operation is called 81 modulo 72. Although you may not realize it, you perform modulo arithmetic when you solve problems involving time. For example, 8 hours from 9 a.m. is 5 p.m. because the hours start over again after they reach 12.

Try using modulo arithmetic to create a new string art design. Cut out another version of the template, but this time connect slits 1 and 3, 2 and 6, 3 and 9, and so forth. The curve that you've created is as beautiful as the cardioid, but carries the unfortunate name of nephroid, meaning "kidney-shaped." This curve shows up in a surprising place. When you look inside a coffee mug, you can see part of a nephroid formed by the reflected light there.

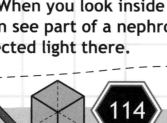

Make String Art Parabolas

By connecting evenly spaced points on two lines, you can create a parabola.

1 Photocopy and cut out a square from the template on page 110. Use boxboard.

2 Cut a short slit at each mark around the perimeter of the square.

3 Tape one end of the thread to the back of the square. Pull the thread around from the back and up through the top slit on the left-hand side of the square, and then down through the first slit on the bottom of the square.

4 Pull the thread up through the second slit on the bottom of the square, and then down through the second slit from the top on the left-hand side.

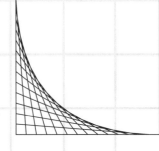

5 Continue this process until you have used up all the slits on the left-hand and bottom sides of the square. The curve you have created is a parabola.

6 If you want, you can repeat steps 3 through 5, using a second thread color, on the other sides of the square to create interesting designs.

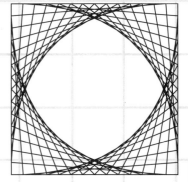

Supplies

- boxboard
- scissors
- craft thread
- tape

Bubbles ✲

People have been playing with bubbles for hundreds of years, and most people are content to blow bubbles for fun. We'll discover their secrets. Don't worry that this will ruin the fun, though. The more you know about bubbles, the more amazed you'll be by them.

OOOOOOOOOOOOOOOOOOOOO

Leonardo da Vinci studied bubbles 500 years ago, describing some of their properties in his notebooks. However, the figure who probably interested the most people in the math and science of bubbles is Charles Vernon Boys. In 1890, Boys wrote a book about experiments with soap bubbles that became a classic for generations of children.

A few simple mathematical rules determine the shapes of bubbles. Surface tension pulls soap film into the smallest possible area. Bubbles are spherical, for example, because a sphere is the shape with the smallest surface area that is capable of holding the air trapped inside.

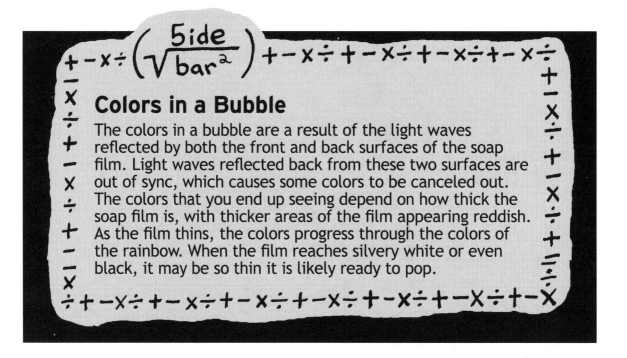

Colors in a Bubble

The colors in a bubble are a result of the light waves reflected by both the front and back surfaces of the soap film. Light waves reflected back from these two surfaces are out of sync, which causes some colors to be canceled out. The colors that you end up seeing depend on how thick the soap film is, with thicker areas of the film appearing reddish. As the film thins, the colors progress through the colors of the rainbow. When the film reaches silvery white or even black, it may be so thin it is likely ready to pop.

When two bubbles join, they create a more complex shape, but the same rule applies. Bubbles naturally solve this math problem every time they arise. However, it has taken mathematicians a long time to catch up to the power of bubble math. They didn't prove that a double bubble is indeed the shape with the smallest surface area for two joined bubbles until the year 2000.

When you dip a bubble wand with a circular opening into bubble solution and then pull it out again, the soap film forms a flat disk in the wand, exactly the shape that you might expect. What if the wand were bent or fashioned into a different shape? You might be surprised at what shape the bubble film takes as it minimizes its surface area.

more on the Web

Make Mathematical Bubble Films

1 Pour the bubble solution into the bowl so that the solution is about 4 inches (10 centimeters) deep.

2 Construct different shapes out of craft wire to dip into the solution. For example, try making a tetrahedron, a cube, and a corkscrew with a wire going down the middle.

3 Dip the shapes into the bubble solution and slowly pull them out to see how the soap film connects the edges of the shapes.

Supplies

- 2 quarts (2 liters) commercial bubble solution
- large bowl
- craft wire
- wire cutters

You can make your own bubble solution by mixing:
- o 9 cups water (2 liters)
- o 1 cup dish detergent (250 milliliters)
- o ¼ cup (60 milliliters) glycerin or corn syrup

Create a Catenoid

more on the Web

You might expect the soap film connecting two circles to go straight from one circle to the other, forming a cylinder between them. Try it and see what shape you get.

1 Create two circles of equal size with handles out of wire. Dip both circles into the bubble solution and then pull them out.

2 Touch the two circles together so their soap films join together.

3 Slowly pull the circles about 1 inch (3 centimeters) apart, and then pop the flat disk cutting across the middle of the surface. The soap film should go from one circle to the other.

4 Continue slowly pulling the circles apart to observe the shape of the soap film.

Supplies

- bubble solution
- craft wire
- wire cutters

The surface that connects the two circles isn't a cylinder, after all. It narrows in the middle, forming a surface called a catenoid, the shape you would get if you rotated a catenary. Until recently, the catenoid was one of only a few known surfaces with minimal surface area. Other members of this group include the plane and the helicoid. A helicoid is the bubble film created by a corkscrew-shaped wire that looks like a spiral staircase or DNA molecule. Today, mathematicians know of all sorts of exotic-looking minimal surfaces.

Discover Patterns in Bubbles

more on the Web

In this activity, you will discover some rules that control the angles at which bubble films meet.

1 Remove the paper labels and the plastic tray that the CD snaps onto from the CD case.

2 Pour bubble solution into a shallow pan. Stand the empty CD case vertically in the bubble solution, so that the open slot in the case is in the bubble solution.

3 Place a straw at the bottom of the CD case, and use it to blow bubbles into the case. Look closely at the bubbles and see if you can discover any patterns in how they come together. How many bubbles meet at any point? What angles do you see?

Supplies

- empty CD case (normal thickness)
- bubble solution
- shallow container
- drinking straw

Did you notice that no more than three bubbles meet at any point, and that, wherever they meet, the angles at which they do so are the same? For example, wherever three bubbles meet, they make three 120-degree angles. It may seem like there are some exceptions to this rule at first glance, but if you look very closely right where the bubbles meet, you will see that it holds true. The reason why the bubbles join with each other in this way is simple: air pressure is the same everywhere inside the bubble foam. Since the forces acting on the bubbles are the same, the angles at which they meet will be the same, too.

120

✿ Snowflakes

Snowflakes are beautiful examples of symmetry in nature. An ideal snowflake has six points, and looks exactly the same rotated to any angle that is a multiple of 60 degrees or reflected in a mirror placed on a line of symmetry.

WORDS + 2 + KNOW

symmetry: the property of a shape that looks the same if you rotate it or look at it in a mirror.

Like a regular hexagon, an ideal snowflake has six lines of symmetry. Look at this picture of the snowflake. Can you determine where its lines of symmetry are? (See page 132 for the answer.)

Snowflakes have six points because the water molecules inside an ice crystal naturally arrange themselves according to hexagonal symmetry. A snowflake often starts out as a hexagon. As more water molecules join the snowflake, however, they attach themselves to the pointy parts of the crystal more quickly, which causes those parts to grow faster. Soon, the familiar shape of a snowflake emerges.

OH! So that's a Koch Snowflake!

$$+ -x \div \left(\frac{5ide}{\sqrt{bar^2}} \right) + -x \div$$

Koch Snowflake

A special shape called a Koch snowflake has a perimeter that is infinitely long! You can make this shape by starting with an equilateral triangle. Erase the middle third of each side of the triangle, and then draw two new segments that point outward like a new, smaller equilateral triangle in the blank space. Repeat this process again with each new line segment. With each step, the shape looks more and more like a snowflake and the perimeter gets longer and longer. If you repeat this process enough times, you can get a perimeter as long as you'd like.

This type of shape is called a fractal because each section of the curve resembles a larger section of the shape, just at a different scale. In other words, if you "zoom in" on any small bump, you will find that it has smaller bumps on it and so on.

Make a Paper Snowflake

more on the Web

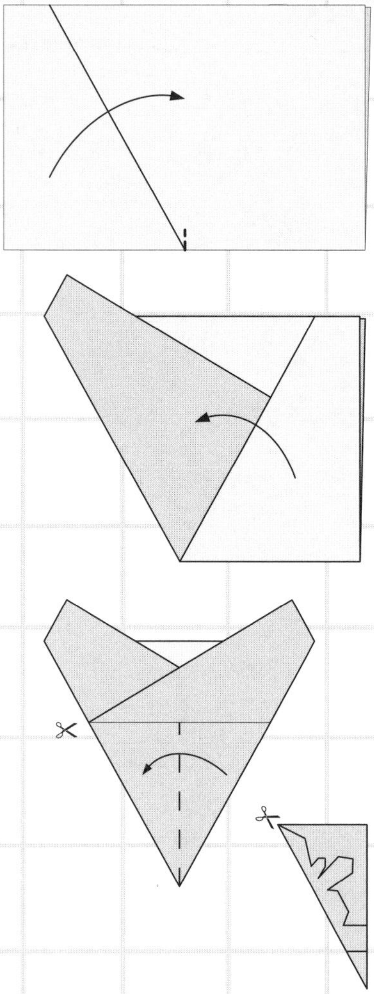

1 Fold a piece of paper in half. Fold it in half again just enough to make a small crease mark at the middle of the folded edge.

2 Fold the paper at 60-degree angles. If you don't have a protractor to measure the angles, just try folding it in thirds.

3 Cut off the extra paper horizontally, starting from one corner. Fold the paper in half along the dashed vertical line.

4 Cut a zigzag out of the paper. Then open it up to see your beautiful creation.

Supplies

- paper
- scissors
- protractor (optional)

Did you know?

You exhale water vapor every time you breathe. The scientist Kenneth G. Libbrecht estimates that roughly 1,000 water molecules from your breath are in each snowflake.

Distorted Images ✺

If you look at yourself in a fun-house mirror, you will see your image distorted in strange ways. One mirror might make you look tall and skinny, while another might make you look short and fat.

OOOOOOOOOOOOOOOOOOOO

Distorted images like these aren't just for fun. Understanding how to transform images is an essential skill for mapmakers and artists. In order to represent the countries of a round world on a flat map, mapmakers must distort the countries' shapes and/or sizes. Painters distort the scenes they create to make them look three-dimensional on a two-dimensional canvas. To show depth, painters must make objects in the background smaller than identical objects in the foreground, and draw lines that are parallel in real life coming together as they recede.

WORDS + **2** + KNOW

anamorphic image: a distorted image that can be restored to its original form by looking at it in a particular way.

Anamorphic images are images that are distorted in such a way that you can see the original, undistorted images if you look at them from a certain perspective or in a specially shaped mirror.

Look at the tall image on this page. It spells a word that you can read if you look at the image from a low angle. Hold this book flat, almost at eye level. What word can you see?

Anamorphic images are used for traffic markings on pavement. When you are riding your bike on a bicycle path, you might see the symbol for a bicycle painted on the path. While the symbol might appear normal to you, it seems so because you are looked at it from a low angle. If you looked down on the image from directly above it, you would see that it is intentionally stretched.

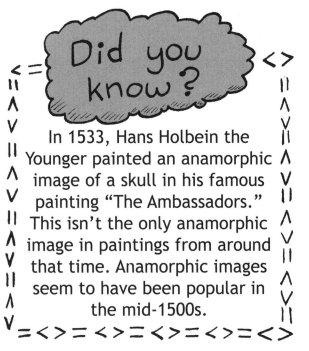

Did you know?

In 1533, Hans Holbein the Younger painted an anamorphic image of a skull in his famous painting "The Ambassadors." This isn't the only anamorphic image in paintings from around that time. Anamorphic images seem to have been popular in the mid-1500s.

Make Anamorphic Art on a Cone

In this activity, you will create a type of anamorphic art on a cone.

Supplies

- paper
- scissors
- tape or glue

1 Photocopy and cut out the template. Roll the template into a cone with the distorted picture of the horse on the outside of the cone.

2 Glue or tape the tab to the edge to form a cone. Look straight down on the cone to see the horse in its original shape.

Draw Your Own Anamorphic Art

more on the Web

In this activity, you will draw your own anamorphic art.

1 Photocopy the circular and semicircular grids in the template.

2 Draw a simple image on the circular grid paper. Transfer each section of your image into the corresponding section on the semicircular grid. You will need to stretch and/or compress the image in each section to fit the new section.

3 Cut out the semicircular grid. Roll up the paper into a cone and tape the tab to the other edge.

4 Look straight down on the cone to see your image.

Supplies

- paper
- pencil
- scissors
- tape

127

Tilings and Patterns ✡

Patterns are all around us. Wallpaper designs, decorative tile patterns, and patterns on clothes can be made by repeating a shape or design to cover a larger area. A pattern made from simple shapes that are shifted, rotated, or reflected to cover an area is called a tiling or tessellation.

○○○○○○○○○○○○○○○○○○○○

The pattern that you probably see most frequently is one made from a grid of squares. You can also create a tessellation out of equilateral triangles or regular hexagons. These three polygons are the only regular polygons capable of tiling a plane themselves.

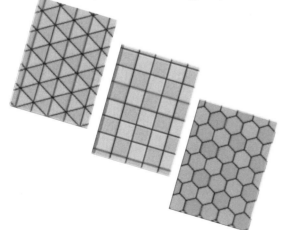

WORDS + 2 + KNOW

tiling: a pattern made from simple shapes that are repeated to cover a plane without gaps or overlaps.

tessellation: a tiling of a plane with regular polygons.

Design Your Own Tiling Pattern

If you don't restrict yourself to regular polygons, you can make many more interesting patterns. Any triangle or any quadrilateral will tile a plane, even oddly shaped ones. Design your own quadrilateral, and then cut out many copies to see how they fit together to make a tiling. To create even more elaborate designs, you can alter a shape that you know tessellates. As long as you follow some basic rules in making your changes, the new shape you create will also tile the plane.

Supplies

- card stock
- a pencil
- scissors
- paper

1 Cut out a square from card stock. Draw a curve that goes from the top left-hand corner to the bottom left-hand corner of the square. You can make any type of curve you like – it doesn't matter how wiggly!

2 Cut along the curve and tape the piece you cut off to the right-hand side of the square, without flipping it upside down.

3 Repeat Steps 2 and 3 with the two other sides of the square. Use this piece as a template to trace many copies onto a piece of paper.

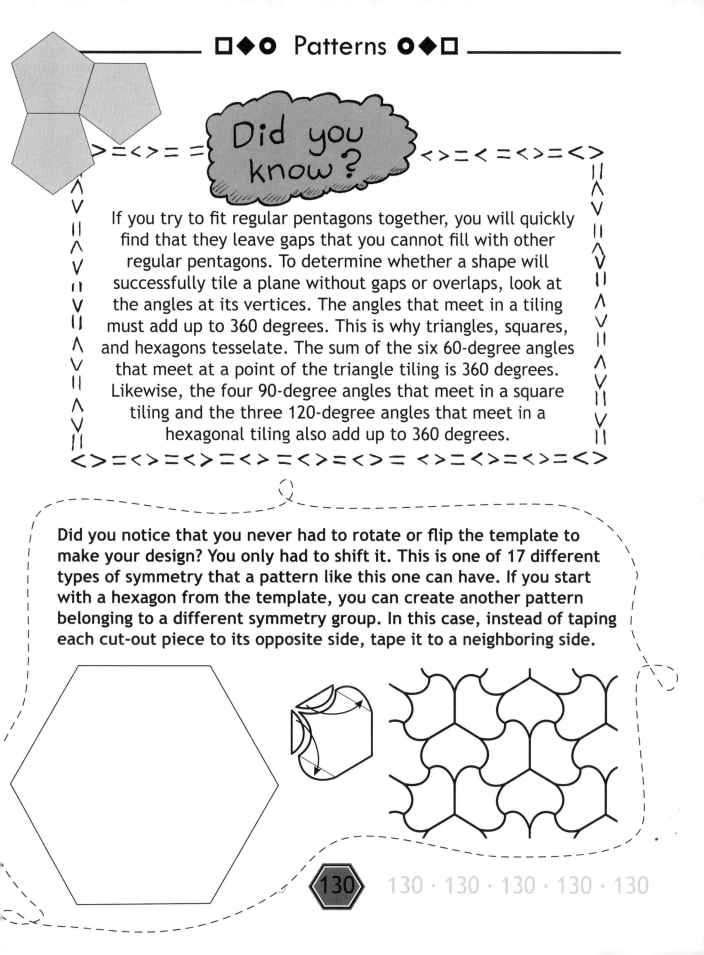

Did you know?

If you try to fit regular pentagons together, you will quickly find that they leave gaps that you cannot fill with other regular pentagons. To determine whether a shape will successfully tile a plane without gaps or overlaps, look at the angles at its vertices. The angles that meet in a tiling must add up to 360 degrees. This is why triangles, squares, and hexagons tessellate. The sum of the six 60-degree angles that meet at a point of the triangle tiling is 360 degrees. Likewise, the four 90-degree angles that meet in a square tiling and the three 120-degree angles that meet in a hexagonal tiling also add up to 360 degrees.

Did you notice that you never had to rotate or flip the template to make your design? You only had to shift it. This is one of 17 different types of symmetry that a pattern like this one can have. If you start with a hexagon from the template, you can create another pattern belonging to a different symmetry group. In this case, instead of taping each cut-out piece to its opposite side, tape it to a neighboring side.

Solutions

Page 8: 1) 45¢ is 1 quarter, 4 nickels, and 0 pennies, so the number $45_{base\text{-}10}$ is written as $140_{base\text{-}5}$. The number $124_{base\text{-}10}$ is written $444_{base\text{-}5}$.

2) The number $314_{base\text{-}5}$ is $84_{base\text{-}10}$, so you would have 84¢.

3) The number $1000_{base\text{-}5}$ is $125_{base\text{-}10}$.

Page 16:

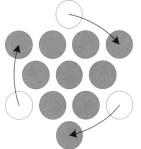

Page 22: 28 is a perfect number because $1 + 2 + 4 + 7 + 14 = 28$. The first few perfect numbers are 6; 28; 496; 8,128; 33,550,336; and 8,589,869,056.

Page 28: The mysteriously appearing square is an illusion. The answer lies in the fact that the pieces don't fit together perfectly to make a rectangle. They leave a small gap with the area of 1 square. This trick uses the Fibonacci numbers 3, 5, and 8, but you can use

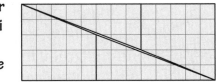

the other Fibonacci numbers to create puzzles, as well. If you cut apart and rearrange a 13 by 13 square into an 8 by 21 rectangle, 1 square seems to disappear.

Page 30: Here are examples of three other spirals that appear in the drawing of a sunflower. There are a Fibonacci number of spirals like these in the drawing: 13, 21, and 89 spirals respectively.

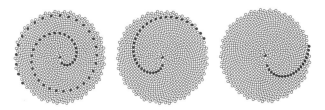

Page 55: You can connect nine dots with four straight lines.

If you "cheat" and make fat dots, you can connect them with only three lines.

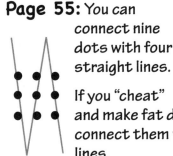

Page 56: The box with an "X" in it is impossible to draw without lifting your pencil. You can see this is true because four vertices have an odd number of edges connected to them. Adding the roof makes it possible, but only if you start at one of the two bottom corners.

Page 57: There is no path that goes through all doors. The graph of the problem shows that there are too many vertices with an odd number of edges.

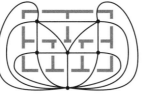

Page 59: The thicker line is the random walk.

Page 64: The first shoelace pattern is the shortest of the three. It has a length of 30.83 centimeters. The second pattern has a length of 32.3 centimeters, and the third pattern has a length of 32.6 centimeters.

Page 65: The longest lacings are:

Here are two more that are not quite as long, but still make a complicated pattern that might be fun to try.

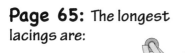

Page 90: Here is how to arrange the two puzzle pieces to form a tetrahedron.

Page 95: Slip one rectangle partially into the slot of another.

Slip the third rectangle (the one with the extra cut) into the slot with the extra cut facing the first rectangle.

Curl tabs out of the way and slide both rectangles the rest of the way into the slot.

Bend the tabs back into place.

Page 121: This snowflake would look the same if you reflected it in a mirror placed on any of the six dashed lines.

Glossary

abacus: an instrument used to perform calculations by moving beads.

anamorphic image: a distorted image that can be restored to its original form by looking at it in a particular way.

base (of a pyramid): the bottom face of a pyramid, the one that doesn't meet at the point where the other faces meet.

base-10: a number system with 10 digits, the numbers 0 through 9.

binary: a base-2 number system (digits 0 and 1), used by computers to store data.

catenary: a curve that is the shape of a hanging chain.

catenoid: a surface formed by rotating a catenary.

circumference: the distance around a circle.

composite: any number greater than 1 that is not a prime number.

concave: curved inward like a bowl or the letter "C."

conic section: a curve that is a cross section of a cone: a circle, ellipse, parabola, or hyperbola.

consecutive: one after another in a list.

cross section: the two-dimensional shape you would see if you were to cut a three-dimensional object in two with one straight cut.

cube: to cube a number is to multiply a number by itself and then by itself again. For example, 4 cubed (written 4^3) is $4 \times 4 \times 4 = 64$. Also a Platonic solid with six square faces.

decagon: a 10-sided polygon.

decimal: a base-10 number system (digits 0 through 9).

diameter: a straight line running from one side of a circle to the other through the center.

diffusion: mixing of molecules due to random movements.

digit: a symbol used to write a number.

dimensions: different directions that you can measure. A line is a one-dimensional object because it can only be measured in terms of its length. A rectangle is a two-dimensional object because it can be measured in terms of its length and width. A cube is a three-dimensional object because it has length, width, and depth.

dodecahedron: a Platonic solid with 12 pentagonal faces.

dual: a solid that fits into another solid with each vertex touching the center of the other solid's faces.

earthly bead: a bead on an abacus with a value of 1.

edge (of a graph): a line that connects two vertices of a graph that represents their relationship.

ellipse: an oval-shaped curve that is a cross section of a cone.

ellipsoid: a solid with elliptical cross sections.

equilateral triangle: a triangle with all sides of equal length.

face: a flat surface on a solid.

factor: a number that divides evenly into another number. For example, the numbers 1, 2, 3, 4, 6, and 12 are factors of 12. To factor a number is to find the numbers that divide evenly into that number.

Fibonacci sequence: a series of numbers formed by adding the previous two numbers to get the next one.

focus (of a parabola): the point inside a parabolic reflector where incoming light rays meet.

focus (of an ellipse): the points that define an ellipse. Waves that start at one focus and reflect inside an ellipse meet at the other focus. The plural of focus is foci.

geodesic dome: a dome built out of triangles to approximate a part of a sphere.

geometry: the study of shapes and their properties.

golden ratio: the number $(1+\sqrt{5})\div2$ or approximately 1.61803, sometimes represented by the Greek letter φ.

golden rectangle: a rectangle with a ratio of its length to width of φ to 1.

graph: a diagram used to analyze the relationships or connections between different things.

heavenly bead: a bead on an abacus with a value of 5.

helicoid: a surface that looks like a spiral staircase or a DNA molecule.

heptagon: a seven-sided polygon.

hexadecimal: a base-16 number system (digits 0 through 9 and letters A through F).

hexagon: a six-sided polygon.

hyperbola: a curve with two branches formed by cutting a double cone.

hyperbolic paraboloid: a surface with parabolas and hyperbolas for cross sections.

hyperboloid of one sheet: a surface formed by rotating a hyperbola.

hypotenuse: the longest side of a right triangle.

icosahedron: a Platonic solid with 20 triangular faces.

inclinometer: an instrument for measuring angles.

integer: a whole number, a number that does not include a fraction.

irrational number: a number that cannot be written as a fraction.

leg: either of the two shorter sides of a right triangle.

mathematician: an expert in math.

modulo: the remainder of a division. For example, 11 modulo 3 is 2.

nonagon: a nine-sided polygon.

octagon: an eight-sided polygon.

octahedron: a Platonic solid with eight triangular faces.

octal: a base-8 number system (digits 0 through 7).

parabola: a U-shaped curve that is a cross section of a cone.

paraboloid: a dish-shaped surface made by rotating a parabola.

parallelogram: a quadrilateral (four-sided shape) whose opposite sides are parallel.

pentagon: a five-sided polygon.

perfect number: a number whose factors (excluding the number itself) add up to that number.

perfect square: a number that is the square of an integer.

plane: a flat surface that extends forever.

Platonic solids: the five solids made up of regular polygons with the same number of faces meeting at each vertex. The Platonic solids are the tetrahedron, cube, octahedron, dodecahedron, and icosahedron.

polygon: a shape on a plane made up of line segments.

polyhedra: the plural of polyhedron, which is a solid formed with polygons as faces.

prime number: a number larger than 1 with only two factors: 1 and itself. The number 1 is not a prime number.

probability: how likely it is, mathematically, that something will happen.

product: the result of multiplying numbers.

protractor: a device for drawing and measuring angles.

pyramid: a solid with a polygon for a base and triangles that meet at a point for all the other faces.

Pythagorean theorem: an equation relating the side lengths of a right triangle.

quadrilateral: a four-sided polygon.

radius: the distance from the center of a circle to any point on the circle.

random walk: a path whose steps are taken in random directions.

ratio: a comparison of two numbers or measurements, dividing one number by another.

regular pentagon: a five-sided regular polygon.

regular polygon: a polygon with each side the same length and each angle the same size.

right angle: a 90-degree angle.

right triangle: a triangle with a right angle in it.

Sieve of Eratosthenes: a method for finding prime numbers.

solid: a three-dimensional geometric shape.

sorobon: a Japanese abacus.

spherical: shaped round, like a sphere.

square: to square a number is to multiply a number by itself. For example 5 squared (written 5^2) is $5 \times 5 = 25$

square root: a number that is squared to produce the original number. For example, the square root of 9 (written $\sqrt{9}$) is 3. $3^2 = 9$.

star polygon: a star formed by connecting every other (or third, fourth, etc.) vertex of a regular polygon.

sum: the result of adding items together (the total).

symmetrical: a property of a shape that looks the same if you rotate it or look at it in a mirror.

symmetry: the property of a shape that looks the same if you rotate it, slide it, or look at it in a mirror.

tessellation: a tiling of a plane with regular polygons.

tetrahedron: a Platonic solid with four triangular faces.

tiling: a pattern made from simple shapes that are repeated to cover a plane without gaps or overlaps.

triangular number: a number of items that can be arranged into rows to form a triangle.

triangle: a three-sided polygon.

vertex (of a graph): a dot on a graph that represents a place or a thing that you are studying. The plural of vertex is vertices.

vertex (of a parabola): the lowest point of a parabola that opens up like a "U."

vertex (of a polygon): a corner point.

volume: the amount of space an object takes up.

Bibliography

Anderson, Marlow, Victor J Katz, and Robin J Wilson, eds. 2004. *Sherlock Holmes in Babylon: And Other Tales of Mathematical History*. Washington, DC: Mathematical Association of America.

Annal, David, and Seth Bareiss. Tessellations - Escher and how to make your own. *Tessellations*. http://www.tessellations.org/.

Bell, Alexander Graham. 1903. Tetrahedral Principle in Kite Structure. *National Geographic Magazine*, June. http://www.fang-den-wind.de/bell_eng.htm.

Berlinghoff, William P. 2004. *Math Through the Ages: A Gentle History for Teachers and Others*. Expanded ed. Washington, DC: Mathematical Association of America.

Blatner, David. 1997. *The Joy of π*. New York: Walker & Co.

Boys, C. V. 1959. *Soap Bubbles and the Forces Which Mould Them*. 1st ed. Garden City, N.Y: Doubleday Anchor Books.

Bradley, Robert E, and Charles Edward Sandifer, eds. 2007. *Leonhard Euler: Life, Work and Legacy*. 1st ed. Amsterdam: Elsevier.

Chyatte, Jeff. 2009. Math and the Arts: Just Passing Through. *Math Horizons* (April): 16.

Cooke, Roger. 2005. *The History of Mathematics: A Brief Course*. 2nd ed. Hoboken, N.J: Wiley-Interscience.

Cromwell, Peter R. 1997. *Polyhedra*. Cambridge, U.K: Cambridge University Press.

Eagle, M. Ruth. 1995. *Exploring Mathematics Through History*. Cambridge: Cambridge University Press.

Fibonacci, Leonardo. 2002. *Fibonacci's Liber Abaci: A Translation into Modern English of Leonardo Pisano's Book of Calculation*. Trans. L. E Sigler. New York: Springer.

Foister, Susan, and National Gallery (Great Britain). 1997. *Holbein's Ambassadors*. London: National Gallery Publications.

Higgins, Peter M. 2007. *Nets, Puzzles, and Postmen*. Oxford: Oxford University Press.

Hopkins, Brian, and Robin J. Wilson. 2004. The Truth about Königsberg. *The College Mathematics Journal 35*, no. 3 (May): 198-207. doi:10.2307/4146895.

Hunt, J. L., B. G. Nickel, and Christian Gigault. 2000. Anamorphic images. *American Journal of Physics 68*, no. 3 (March): 232-237.

Isenberg, Cyril. 1978. *The Science of Soap Films and Soap Bubbles*. Clevedon: Tieto Ltd.

Libbrecht, Kenneth George. 2003. *The Snowflake: Winter's Secret Beauty*. Stillwater, MN: Voyageur Press.

Liungman, Carl G. Symbols.com - Symbol 28:24. *Online Encyclopedia of Western Signs and Ideograms*. http://www.symbols.com/encyclopedia/28/2824.html.

Livio, Mario. 2003. *The Golden Ratio: The Story of Phi, the World's Most Astonishing Number*. 1st ed. New York: Broadway Books.

Lovett, D. R, and NetLibrary, Inc. 1994. *Demonstrating Science with Soap Films*. Bristol: Institute of Physics Pub.

Maor, Eli. 2007. The Pythagorean *Theorem: A 4,000-Year History*. Princeton: Princeton University Press.

Mitchison, G. J. 1977. Phyllotaxis and the Fibonacci Series. *Science 196*, no. 4287. New Series (April 15): 270-275. doi:10.2307/1743115.

Mungan, I., and Udo Wittek. 2004. *Natural draught cooling towers*. Taylor & Francis, April 15.

Myers, Gardiner H. *Shapes of Molecules*. http://www.chem.ufl.edu/~myers/chm2045/shapes.htm.

Naylor, Michael. 2002. Golden, Square Root of 2, and π Flowers: A Spiral Story. *Mathematics Magazine 75*, no. 3 (June): 163-172. doi:10.2307/3219239.

Pickover, Clifford A. 2006. *The Möbius Strip: Dr. August Möbius's Marvelous Band in Mathematics, Games, Literature, Art, Technology, and Cosmology.* New York: Thunder's Mouth Press.

Polster, Burkard. 2006. *The Shoelace Book: A Mathematical Guide to the Best (and worst) Ways to Lace Your Shoes.* Providence, R.I: American Mathematical Society.

Pugh, Anthony. 1976. *Polyhedra: A Visual Approach.* Berkeley: University of California Press.

Rudman, Peter Strom. 2007. *How Mathematics Happened: The First 50,000 Years.* Amherst, N.Y: Prometheus Books.

Sayili, Aydin. 1960. Thâbit ibn Qurra's Generalization of the Pythagorean Theorem. *Isis 51*, no. 1 (March): 35-37. doi:10.2307/227603.

Stewart, Ian. 2007. *Game, Set and Math: Enigmas and Conundrums.* Mineola, N.Y: Dover Publications.

Strain, Steve. *Golden Ratio Dividers. Wolfram Demonstrations Project.* http://demonstrations.wolfram.com/GoldenRatioDividers/.

Williams, Michael R. 1985. *A History of Computing Technology.* Englewood Cliffs, N.J: Prentice-Hall.

Woodburn, Glenda. *Tetrahedral Kite Building Instructions.* http://web.archive.org/web/20070501184645/gw011.k12.sd.us/building.htm.

Index